Positive Programming

The **Secret** Key to

Releasing Anxiety &
Finding Internal

Happiness

Positive Programming
The Secret Key to Releasing Anxiety & Finding Internal Happiness

©Emma Jayne Taylor

2021 Edition

Disclaimer

My personal story is given in order to explain my discoveries, with the intention to help others. If you are concerned in any way about your mental health, then please speak with your health provider.

I know that the *natural* methods in this book work for *me*, which is why I feel the need to share these with others who could potentially benefit from them.

It was my choice to take the actions I decided upon in order to heal my mind and body, and at my own risk. I would always advise everyone to seek medical help before taking advice from *any* book, including this one.

<u>I am Declaring that...</u>

I cannot delve into everybody's personal circumstances such as money, work, health, relationships - but I can tell you how-to practice a good mind-set! It is up to *you*, as an individual to practice the methods in this book in order to create a happier life for yourself!

Joy

I believe the ultimate success in life is finding genuine, internal **joy**!
If you have joy in your life, then you are fulfilling every aspect of your desires. You are on the right track!
If you are lacking joy, then you need to discover the mastery of your own mind, and as a result – your life!

The *control* centres of this life are the <u>mind</u>, <u>physical body</u> and our <u>energy body</u> (otherwise known as the "spirit" or "ethereal" body).
I am a great example of a cure to severe, generalised anxiety and depression, having found these three connections.

I re-programmed my mind naturally in order to manage mental health, and fixed my body from painful habits, using the three main parts: -

The mind =   Thoughts, words & beliefs
The physical body =   Actions
The energy body =   Feelings

Finding your "whole self" is a wonderful journey of *re-membering* yourself. It is an amazing combination chosen by us in order to *create* on an Earthly plane. If we know this, then we can focus on making it amazingly exciting and wonderful for us!
This life is yours! Make it so!

~ 4 ~

My Story

Please bear with me for the first part of this book. My story is truly relevant, as it was such a transformation from extreme and seemingly uncontrollable fear and sadness. The growth I have experienced beyond what I thought was humanly possible was so incredible. It was literally a battle with "the self" for a few years! I now know that every "suffering" brings opportunity! I know that the lessons learnt from mental health concerns were an amazing opportunity for growth!
I wish to carry forward my experiences in order to help *you*, and many others!

Approximately 11 years ago, I ultimately discovered the connection between mind, body and energy, realising the vital importance of this for overall (and holistic) health. This discovery was the only way I was ever going to recover from an unexpected mental health "break-down."
Like many people, I thought I was a fit, healthy, invincible human being!
With this break-down, I thought that severe anxiety and depression would eventually take my life, even if it were me that would have made that ultimate decision.
Now, I want to keep *that* terribly negative side of my experience very brief, as this is a book about positivity!
I now know that life is an amazing gift and ultimately needs to be lived! We all have our Soul purpose!

I just wanted you to know that I was as bad as anyone could get in terms of anxiety and depression. I can only describe it as being in a constant state of fear and panic, with emotions that I appeared to have no control over. My heart was forever beating too hard and too rapidly, making my body so rigid and unable to relax; my mind was constantly racing and unable to focus on one particular thing; I had forgotten *who* I actually was as a character; there wasn't an ounce of sleep, and my routines were *forced*, simply to remain alive. I felt at one point as if my mind had switched off and reset itself, leaving me in a primitive state. There were also times that I felt the curtains were closing in on me and that my heart had stopped, with difficulty getting the heart rate back. I believe I was mentally and physically exhausted and lucky to have made it through.

Medics would have said that I *should* have been in a mental health ward, pumped full of medication, but I decided to tackle this on my own (somehow!).

The only thing keeping me focussed was the fact that I had thirty-seven years of practical thinking behind me.
I realised that I somehow created this situation, so I knew deep down that I needed to "un-create" it and recreate myself anew!

One turning point for me was when I was deep into the situation. I was lying in bed, trying to find a way to go to sleep – yet again! For some reason I had a second's worth of courage in my mind. During that moment of time, my heartbeat calmed for a few beats. It was at that specific point of realisation that I needed to find a way of retaining *that* **courage** somehow! It made me recognise the huge connection between mind and body – and reversely, body and mind!

This was not my *only* discovery, as at another point in time (during the thick of it) I noticed signs and guidance that made me question life as a whole! These signs made me realise that everything is energy!

Life is magical and is such a great opportunity with this combination of mind, body and energy.
This mind uses the intention through choices; the body is our set of tools to complete the actions as a result; and our energy interacts, allowing a creation with the energy we put out and receive. We are here to manifest and create!
I created my own set of circumstances – we all do!

With all of the above and more, I have discovered the secret to a happy life!
Let me run through it stage by stage in this book, hoping that you too, can find **your** ultimate happiness.

I Needed a Diagnosis

This is an important topic to share, as many people find themselves confused with the symptoms of anxiety or depression. Again, I am just adding my part should it be helpful to compare to...

When my condition began, I believed it was a *physical* concern. Doctors initially checked my heart function and general wellbeing. Thankfully, after some time, they could not find anything physically wrong with me (after ECG's and a heart monitor!).
After several visits to the doctors and A&E, I eventually understood and *accepted* that it was a mental health concern.
During those particular days, mental health didn't appear to have much support. I was told to speak to my General Practitioner, who guided me to a councillor. I attended one session and felt too nervous to return, as I did not feel as if this person could help me.

Today, I know that mental health is most certainly widely recognised. I would always advise that you speak to your health practitioner initially. A diagnosis is important in order to understand *any* condition.
Once you know what is wrong with you, you can make things right!

Once I knew what was happening to me, I knew that it was *me* that created the situation. I wanted to reverse, or re-train my mind somehow. At this point I didn't know *how*, but I wondered if the *opposite* actions could reverse the effects. If I had filled my mind with fear and negative thoughts and predictions, then my idea was that I could fill my mind with love, comfort and positive thoughts, always looking at a solution instead of focussing on the problems.

This was *one* of my important starting points.

Over time I calculated the effects of thought and emotion on the mind, body and energy.

So, with this in mind, I hope that this book will help you immensely!

<u>I Created This Situation for Myself</u>

So, I know that I have already explained the personal realisation that I "got myself into this mess" and that I somehow knew that I could "un-create" this mess. This turned out to be completely and utterly true!

Let me reveal the first secret: **You *can* heal yourself!**
We create our own circumstances with our thoughts, words, beliefs and actions, which in turn gives out a particular energy, which attracts more of the same.
What we put out we get back.
If we create dis-ease, then we receive disease.
If we create ease, then we receive ease.

When I had a look back after a period of time, it was purely evidential that my thoughts and emotions were the cause of my issues. I never knew that somebody could get so *ill* simply from *thinking* and responding to circumstances incorrectly. Thoughts are the *food* of the mind! Thoughts are very real!

Previously, I mentioned that I had an extremely brief moment of realisation that: "courage in the mind created a sense of calm in the body."
At this point, I couldn't seem to simply select a courageous mind-set, as my mind was already programmed into this negative and unhealthy state. I knew that everything I feared was not logical. Those who are very anxious, perhaps with

the Generalised Anxiety condition, say that their fear is "silly", or "stupid," as they know that it is completely irrational.   The truth is that it *isn't* silly or stupid. It is simply because the mind has been programmed to be that way to form a "condition."

It is a bit like walking badly and getting a bad knee, then learning to walk properly to allow the knee to heal!

The mind needs to be "re-programmed" from "**bad**" thinking to "**good**" thinking, in order to feel better in every way. This is just the same as choosing good foods over bad foods.

My "*re-programming*" phrase is simply a way of explanation, for a term that fits my methods extremely well!

This is where the good stuff begins.

These 4 things are important to remember: -

*What we put out in life reflects back to us.

*What we believe, we receive.

*Our thought, spoken word and emotion creates a frequency that attracts the same energy.

*Positive <u>visualisation</u> coupled with <u>intention</u> manipulates energy, for healing or creation.
Add passion for enhanced effects!

YOUR MIND NEEDS YOU TO BE THE MASTER!

This is secret number 2!: You are the master of your own mind!

It is vital to be the kind, gentle, respectful, loving, supporting, encouraging ... best friend of your own mind/self!
This is where you master your life!

Not only does this way of "thinking and speaking" aid your mental health, but it also reflects in your physical wellbeing. The mind-body connection is very real.

It is true and right to love, respect, support or encourage your own "self" without guilt, hatred, resentment or criticism. Love yourself enough to know that **you are worth** all of this love and positivity!
Love and respect yourself with humility, and without condition!
Believe in yourself!
Only accept the same from others and disregard anything that isn't of such compassion, love and respect.

Be the mindful master of your mind.

I personally believe that we are of a "consciousness" and that we speak from this consciousness to our physical minds. Our physical minds allow us to produce thoughts and words that produce an energy, which attracts the same energy in return.

No matter *how* our minds are "built," they are **amazing and powerful**! Although I know we are born with particular gene factors, I also know that as we learn and grow, we have the **power to programme** it in our own unique way. Most of us don't realise we are the master of our own minds!

Your mind is extremely powerful!

It is ***our*** **individual** ***responsibility*** and ***job*** to take care of our minds and to be aware of **what thoughts we feed it with**. It is our job to tell our minds who and how we wish to be, and what we want in life!

You are the master of your own mind, so be kind, gentle, respectful and loving to your own mind. It is your job to take good care of your mind. This reflects in our life and is demonstrative in the actions we take and the life we create.

To think and believe negative thoughts is only creating a battle within the self. Why battle with yourself?
We throw our own hurdles in front of ourselves so many times when it is completely unnecessary. I often look back and realise that I created everything that has manifested, whether through choices (mind), actions (intention and

deliberate movement toward that), emotions/feelings (the frequency we attract).

We can all choose to have peace and love within. It is wonderful to be the positive, loving, gentle master of yourself.

Your mind literally listens to *everything* you tell it, and it believes you!
So do not tell yourself that you are stupid, weak, or useless! Do not allow your mind to accept any negative criticism from anyone else either!
Tell yourself that you are intellectual, strong and a very integral part of this universe! You are! We all have our own set of gifts. We were all created to be unique. If we were all the same, this life wouldn't work for us.

Be the master of your own mind, do not be the slave to other people attempting to master your mind.

If you don't believe in the ability to programme your mind, then think about the example of those who train in the forces. Let us take the Air Force as an example. I have seen people who have trained their minds to be so accurate and particular, that even when they retire, their minds still function with the same habits. Perhaps their tool kits are extremely clean; or their clothes perfectly ironed; the furniture is so specifically placed; or the household items are in a particular lay-out; their punctuality is precise; the daily routines are very regimented.

This behaviour was required for the accuracy of their work, which carries over into "civilian life."

With regards to mental health, people programme their minds with a negative pattern, always saying no to opportunities, or avoiding fun events; believing that they can't do this or that, holding very little self-value, self-love or self-respect; believing they are always ill, or lacking love from others. The vicious circle is that they are always attracting the *same*.

Once people are aware of their patterns, these can literally be broken with a better outlook on themselves and life. A better pattern of thought creates a better mind, and in turn - better health and a much better life!

Some people say to me, "if you tell yourself the opposite of what you seemingly know, then you are lying to yourself, and you won't believe it."

What I *know*, is that we are naturally of LOVE and JOY, therefore when we are treating ourselves with such deliberate thoughts of sadness and negativity, we are not acting in truth or love. It is the negative thought patterns that have been a lie to ourselves. To hold a loving and joyous thought pattern is speaking the truth to ourselves. To reverse the pattern is actually in order to heal ourselves!

A baby will see all of the joy in life and find fun in everything that they see.

I have seen animals full of joy, yet the human behaviour
begins to condition it out of them, just the same as we train
the joy out of ourselves!
We can literally talk the joy out of ourselves and others if we
are not the loving masters of our own minds!
Life has been created in love! We are meant to see the
magic and splendour of life.

So, to condition ourselves with love and joy, holding that
reminder of the magic of life – we have the beautiful cycle of
that behaviour reflecting back to us.

If you can teach yourself the importance of self-love and self-
respect, then it reflects outwardly and attracts the same
energy back towards you.
Once you learn to love and respect yourself, you find such
ease in loving and respecting others, with *understanding*.

To master your mind is to create a strong "core-self" so that
any external factor cannot impact the love and respect you
have for yourself. No matter what happens around you, you
remain internally happy!
See the magic and beauty of life!

Self-Image

Everyone has an image of themselves in their mind.
Some people think very negatively of themselves.
Self-image should be that of love and admiration for the self.
There is no *other* specific, or unique, natural coding of
yourself!
You can learn to love and respect yourself at any point.
Every single day is a new beginning filled with amazing
opportunities!
**In this present moment, huge change can be made by a
single decision!**

Most of us look in the mirror with a critical mind. We can
choose to change our viewpoint.
A great strength is to smile at yourself and tell yourself that
you love yourself and this life so much. Tell yourself that you
are happy - and believe it. After a while, allow the belief to
become a *knowing*. Do this daily for great results over time.
**Complete this act with love and excitement for huge
potential in this wonderful gift of life.**

We manifest *everything* about ourselves, even the way we
appear as a physical being. Isn't that already enough to find
love and respect for who we have chosen ourselves to be?

We are amazing without the labels. If we can see ourselves
as the beautiful beings that we are as a whole, knowing that

we are unique gifts to this planet, then just recognising our true-selves is pure, unconditional love.

If we could all just know how beautiful we are and how amazing our bodies are as "tools," then we wouldn't judge or compare ourselves to those of "celebrity" status. We are all bodies, minds and energy all rolled into one!

Jealousy is just the comparison to others. Love who and what you are, knowing that you are a wonderful gift who can create! If you could see your light of energy, then you would know that you are just as amazingly beautiful as everyone else.

It truly does not matter what other people's perceptions of us are. It is only important to have an amazing perception of *ourselves*. Everyone will always have their own perception no matter what! **To live life, is literally to live life without the opinions of others.**

Please simply love yourself, no matter who you are!

The Mind-Body-Energy Overview

*Our thoughts, beliefs, emotions and actions are food for the mind, body and our energy!

*We are what we digest with all of our senses. We are what we see, hear, smell, taste and sense, and how we interpret and digest this information.

*Our social influences and upbringing can determine our belief systems, but when we begin to think for ourselves, we can choose who and what we wish to be.

Open your mind to new possibilities!

You're probably aware of similar words of wisdom, but I am living evidence that proves these truths.

Before I "fell ill," I didn't have much confidence in myself, or see my personal value. After recovery, I built up confidence and personal value that I never, ever thought I would have!

When I fell ill, I felt as if my mind had "switched off" and "reset" itself. At this point I was extremely sensitive to external information. I felt as if I was reborn into a babies' mind yet dwelling within an adult's body. It felt as if my memory was a "collective spider's web" that someone's

finger had broken through. Thankfully, I was still holding my previous logic and wisdom that had been collected over the 37 years of my life, but my mind felt empty and full of extreme fear of everything. I completely believe that this was a second opportunity to rebuild my mind, but in a more positive and effective way. This was an immense gift!
I noticed my **feelings**, so began to feel connected to what **felt** good... and what **felt** bad. Initially, I avoided all negative/bad things and accepted all good things in order to heal! It was a natural order of things for me. It told me that our minds and bodies prefer the "**good feelings!**"

Feelings are our energy bodies speaking to us.
Good feelings bring balance, comfort and harmony to all parts of our being!
I believe that our feelings guide us.

Everything is energy. We are energy, vibrating in frequencies.

Like-attracts-like!

At this early stage, I was also extremely sensitive to energy generally!
I could feel other people's energy and the energy around me.
I could also *see* the energy around people. There have been signs that have guided me as well.
I shall most certainly be getting into the subject of *energy* as this book unfolds.

Before I understood the mind, body and energy connections, it was quite nerve-wracking in itself to discover these things! This was a time of the already-created fear, coupled with added fear due to things that I couldn't initially understand. I will get into the subject of "fear" later in the book.

The Conscious and Sub-Conscious

There are different perceptions of the conscious and sub-conscious parts of the mind. I like to think about the typical iceberg image.

You see the surface part of the iceberg (conscious mind), which is our current thinking and emotive state – our present tense!

The larger part of the iceberg (being the **sub**conscious – and literal **sub**merged part), is the storage part of the mind, which holds our every experience - everything we have thought about or done. It holds our automatic actions and responses. It is how we can automatically walk up and down stairs without thinking about it, or how we can drive a regular route and forget the detail of how we got to our destination. We have programmed it to respond to events in particular ways. It is effectively our storage and automatic memory bank.

I believe the two parts of the mind work together (naturally!). The subconscious mind has been taught to respond to things in a particular way by our conscious mind (and many, many previous experiences). We can amend our responses to things however, once we hold **awareness**!

The subconscious mind will believe anything you store in it and hold some automatic responses. You can lie to it, and this part of your mind will believe it.

Therefore, it is important to feed your mind with loving, caring, courageous, comforting and positive thought and belief. Create *that* level of **attitude** and keep the good feeling!

I believe that *good* creates an even **greater** *good*!

You can feed your mind with comforting, positive, healthy and loving things, which will help you in life generally; or you can feed your mind with the opposite, which (in my opinion), doesn't bring the best state of mind or body.

I genuinely didn't realise that a negative pattern of thoughts could affect your mind negatively, affecting all parts of the mind, body and energy. It is almost like self-destruction already!

Do not self-destruct!

Choose to **Construct!**

Construct your selected mind-set.

I did not realise that the mind is so specific in the beliefs we give ourselves, and that it acts itself out!

If you keep saying "I forgot" many times, your mind will believe that it keeps forgetting.

If you keep saying "I can't see this/that" then your mind will gradually believe the eyes cannot see that well.

If you keep saying "I can't stand it," then you may even get foot problems! The mind is **very** specific to what you tell it and is aware of everything you do!

Focus on telling yourself the right things.

If I keep cursing to myself with each error made, then my mind listens. If I simply say, "that's typical," then my mind will accept that certain events are typical for me, which isn't

~ 23 ~

always a good thing, unless it's associated with positive events.

If I tell myself that I am so fortunate and lucky, then my mind will believe *that* and attract more of that. What we 'put out we get back.'

What you believe you will receive!

Negative thought patterns will attract more negative thought, belief and feeling.

Positive thought patterns will attract more positivity, belief and feeling. Imagine that amazing *frequency* of positivity!

*Our emotions create a frequency that attracts the same energy.

Visualise for a moment, a moneybox just for comparison-sake.

Imagine you have shiny, gold money (representing loving, positive thought); and black, metal tokens (representing negative self-talk or thought).

Imagine the money box is your mind and you feed it either the black tokens or shiny money. Both fill the money box, but one will bring value to you and the other won't.

How would *you* choose to fill *your* money box? Or mind? It is your choice.

Remember, you are the master of your own mind!

Question: If you know that *time* is the real currency, then how do you want to spend that currency?

~ 24 ~

The submerged/subconscious part of the mind just does exactly what you tell it to do over a period of a collection of thoughts over time.

Think of an injured part of the body that you have subconsciously protected by holding it in a particular way. I can give a good example of this. I dislocated my elbow several times as a child. Each time I dislocated it, it would pop back into the correct position, but then remain at a ninety-degree angle.

When it healed, I could move it normally, but I would still hold it at that ninety-degree angle because my subconscious had trained that part of me to hold that action. My elbow was fine, but the body acted out the protective position continually. I needed to remember that I could move the elbow by practicing a full range of movement and relaxing it into the fully extended position.

This is relative to mind health! When you continually tell yourself (and/or others) that you are anxious or depressed, your mind will believe it and your mind and body will continually act it out with the same patterns. The cycle needs to be broken by practicing new thought-patterns and a new set of beliefs. You can choose to break that cycle *now* with the reprogramming techniques.

Tell yourself daily that you are happy and calm and install that belief! You may not *feel* the results instantly, but over time you will notice the difference.

When calm is more present, then hypnotherapy or meditation can be introduced for specific focus on calm and happiness, gaining deeper access to your subconscious.

Let me tell you that you are not depressed, and you are not anxious. You may *have* depression or anxiety at a particular point in time, but you are not ***that***! The only reason you would *have* that would be due to a certain set of thoughts and beliefs over a period of time. The thoughts and beliefs can affect you in fear, or sadness, by imagining the worst or being stuck in the past.

Negative mind-sets of continual recycling/addictive patterns are feeding your money box with the black tokens!

If you spoke to your friends with negative, criticising, hurtful words continually, then they wouldn't be in your company for long if they had any respect for themselves.

It is valuable to love your own company, as this is a great strength for internal happiness. Just remember that we must be able to live comfortably with ourselves. It is wonderful to have love and confidence in our own thoughts.

The cycle of negative thought and belief needs to be broken and replaced by loving, comforting, respectful thoughts and beliefs, even if it is difficult to begin with! ***Daily practice*** is what is required if negative thinking appears to overpower you. Gradual, daily effort makes it possible to have more loving, positive and comforting thoughts! It is important to know that you need to be **gentle with yourself**!

You deserve happiness, calm and courage in this life! It is simply a choice! Make the change today, do not delay!

Once you know that you are the <u>master</u> of your own mind and that it is your <u>job</u> to take care of your mind, then you will begin to be aware of your thoughts. This is when you can make dramatic changes to your emotions, and as a result – your life!

Are We "Consciousness?"

I know that I have already mentioned my personal belief in our "consciousness" existence and that we interact with our physical brain, which is why I have the theory that our physical mind and body is the tool.

I like to think that if our subconscious is the "listener" and the "absorber" of the thoughts we are feeding it, then we are the ones with the controls, observing all experiences that are exposed, given our thoughts and actions.
With that literally in mind, it's important to live our lives to the fullest, with the choice to observe and *feel* every day.

If we are observers of this life, then we are making choices based on our experiences. We need to *experience* in order to learn, grow and evolve.

"Life is about collecting experiences, with your mind being the only limitation."

To know that we are immortal energy-bodies first, carrying the physical aspects of our mind and body as a clever vessel, then as observers through experiences, we can see this life as an amazing gift that we need to live out.
We all have our perfect imperfections so that we have specific focus on certain experiences. There are no limitations however, so to have *that* mind-set is a super-strength!

Our physical mind and body is temporary, yet so amazing.
We truly need to make the most of this gift!
The present is a gift – literally a present! Live today with
immense gratitude. Each day is a fresh opportunity to
change anything! We are free to make the choices we wish,
as observers of our own experiences.

The Positives and Negatives

*You create your life through your own perception.

We all need "negatives" in order to understand the "positives," otherwise we would not understand one without the other. We have all come here with *perfect imperfections* in order to learn and grow. I like to think of the "negatives" as a particular matter that has been exposed in order to evaluate what we could potentially *work on* in order to grow and evolve. Therefore, any negativity or discomfort is actually a gift! It's wise to focus on all positive aspects in life in order to attract the same, but it is important to know that the opposite has been exposed as a gift to you in order to take the opportunity to grow!

*Discomfort is where growth lies!

*The energy body that we are - communicates by a way of "feelings."

"Negatives" and "Positives" create ***feelings*** within us!
This is where the ***secret*** to a healthy and happy mind comes in...

~ 30 ~

Secret number 3: Our feelings speak to us!

Most people ignore their feelings and move through any
situation without paying attention to them.
How we *feel* projects outward and acts like a magnet to
receiving the same energy in return.
If something feels good, then continue to follow those
thoughts and actions. If you feel the opposite, then it is good
to calculate what *will* bring good feeling.

We attract what we put out.
Think about an actual projector. What is projected on a
screen or wall is played back to us. It's the same perception.
Sometimes it's hard to break the constant record of thoughts
and feelings, but it is worth the gradual practice, building up
amazing change. If you're projecting constant negative
drama and horror back to yourself, then you need to
calculate how to produce happy, joyous, heart-warming
projections.

One example I can give is when I kept injuring myself at one
point, doing silly things. As a result, I kept thinking "I keep
injuring myself," and at the same time I was feeling sorry for
myself. The thoughts, coupled with the feelings I projected,
were only attracting more events that caused me injuries!
Once I realised what I was doing, I told myself all positive
things, such as "that's the final injury," or "things can only get
better now." I have also been known to apologise to myself

for manifesting such things with thought and feeling and to correct it, with new thoughts and feelings.

Our feelings are very much a "live body!"
Some people like to call our "energy body" the *ethereal* or *spiritual* body. I prefer to say that we are pure energy and that our energy-body likes to communicate with us in order to guide us on our journey.
The energy body that we essentially are – is the part that guides us in intuition/our 6th sense. I believe it is our "true self." If all of us listened to this part of ourselves more, then our choices would be the best ones! It is all about trusting yourself!

I have noticed that the most revolutionary movies, or books, are those which are speaking to our energy bodies. They connect with us and make us feel excited.
Some of these movies are those such as Star Wars; The Matrix; Avatar; Inception; Lord of the Rings; or books like Harry Potter. One movie I can highly recommend is "Powder!" There are a lot of truths spoken in this script. This would be the production from 1995.

With *positives* and *negatives* of the mind, there is the common theory based on "which wolf you wish to feed." In the 2007 film "Pathfinder," this is the most abbreviated written quote: -

Starfire: "There are two wolves fighting in each man's heart. One is love, the other is hate."
Ghost: "Which one wins?"
Starfire: "The one you feed the most."

At the end of the day, my strong belief is that we came to *be* for a reason. The reason is to experience, learn and grow, and become our wisest, truest selves. I believe we have come here to work on ourselves for a greater understanding, whilst helping others through their own journey of understanding.
I've always put others first, so during *my* time of personal discovery, it was difficult working on my "inside" world, but once you discover how important *you* are and how you influence others, you realise how working on yourself is important!

There is an old story of a couple of men being stuck in the desert with only one bottle of water. One of the men is gravely injured, so the other man knows he needs to carry him to a hopeful destination for rescue. The journey is quite long, so the person being carried is given some water, but the person carrying the man needs *more* water in order to be helpful and functional for both of them.

~ 33 ~

Details of this story aside – it demonstrates the importance of looking after oneself in order to be helpful to others.
I like my own saying: "you're no good, if you're no good."
Even if you don't set out to be helpful to others, I'm sure most of us wish to be well and inspiring for all of those who love or care about us.

Let's get to the nitty gritty!

Awareness of Our Thoughts and Feelings

If we are aware of our thoughts and how they impact the
way we *feel*, then the benefits are outstanding!
There are two feelings overall. Let's keep it simple. There
are the **good feelings** and the **bad feelings**. The difference is
that the good feelings make us feel *good*, and the bad
feelings make us feel *uncomfortable*.
We don't have to go deeply into subjects of anger, hatred,
jealousy, frustration, sadness (etc.) in order to know that any
of these would be classified as a *bad* feeling.
Or that any feeling of joy, excitement, wellness, love,
comfort, and so forth would be classified as a *good* feeling.

We generally know when something feels comfortable and
when something feels uncomfortable.

It is clear that we need the *bad* feelings in order to
understand that we can feel good!
Allow your feelings to speak to you, as this is their **genuine
purpose!**

Have you ever gone into a situation knowing that it didn't
feel comfortable, but you decided to go ahead with it
anyway? Later down the line you realise there was evidence
that it wasn't the right thing for you to get into or be involved
in?
If something doesn't feel right, then it generally isn't right –
for *you* anyway. What's right for one isn't always right for

another. We are all guided by our own feelings and perceptions! We can change our perceptions in order to create good feelings.

If something brings you comfort with the "good" feelings, then follow *that* feeling.

*Thoughts and Words are The Food to The Mind

Secret number 4: The thoughts and words you select for yourself - feed your mind.

This is vital information. The thoughts and words you select for your mind are all contributing to your beliefs and behaviours.
The type of "food" you put into your mind is how your mind will determine how you feel about yourself. This is where your feelings come in again. If thoughts give you an uncomfortable feeling, then it's your feelings speaking to you. If you become aware of your thoughts and the effects on your feelings, then you can create either a wonderfully comfortable "self", or a very uncomfortable "self."
Again, this is the difference between feeling "good" and feeling "bad."

If you keep telling yourself negative things such as: -

My balance is bad.
My co-ordination is crap.
My memory is rubbish.
I'm not fit.
I'm stupid.
I'm grumpy...

You get the picture...
Your mind and body will believe these things and act these out. If your body and mind acts these things out, then the belief gets strong too. Anything disrespectful or going against your true amazingness will create a negative feeling. Therefore, it's important to listen to your feelings, as they're trying to tell you what works well for you in life!

Instead, tell yourself things such as: -

I am clever (we all have our unique and specific type of intelligence).
I am happy (we can literally *choose* to be happy!).
I am fit!
I have an amazing body!
I am a wonderful person!

Your mind and body will believe these wonderful things and create feelings that are happy and comfortable! Just keep practicing these thoughts.

Thoughts are food for the mind, so keep feeding the mind with good thoughts, a bit like a healthy way-of-eating that will begin to pay off in good time.

Then again, if others tell you that you are stupid, or ugly, or unhealthy, or unfit (and so on), then you have the choice to take that on board or not. Remember that you are the master of your **own** mind! Do not opt to be the slave to other people's minds with their controlling or critical words. I would say have respect enough for yourself, knowing that it is your job to filter in (or out), what words offered to you will be accepted. Only accept the words that will make you *feel* good about yourself. Have respect and love enough for yourself to do this. Have enough respect for yourself to be in the company of those who feed you healthy words and a natural level of love and respect.
If you don't wish to accept particular words, collected as your own thoughts then tell yourself something else!
Understand that those who reflect criticism or negativity on you are still learning and growing. It is likely that they are terribly negative and critical towards themselves. In many ways it is "their mind-set" based on the set of choices they have made for themselves, but it reflects outwardly.
Knowing this is useful in order to still love and forgive everyone. These are usually people who need more love and understanding. Just remember to protect your own mind by being the master of your own thoughts and words, with self-love and respect.

We all need to begin with a good relationship with ourselves.
Our mind is filled with many old thoughts and patterns. We
are also filled with other people's old thoughts.
We are filled with the power of choice and the power of
now! It is time to recreate yourself a-new.
You are your own decision-maker for yourself!
Choose who you wish to be right now.

Our Human Senses

*We are what we digest with all of our senses. We are what we see, hear, smell, taste and sense, and how we interpret and digest this information.

With our physical being, it is important to understand the effects of our senses.
Giving myself as an example, when I was initially "rebuilding" my brain, I noticed I naturally avoided any negative influence.
Negativity of any kind made me feel extremely uncomfortable. This is where I was noticing the mind, body and energy connection.

I couldn't watch the news, any soap opera, dark thriller, any argumentative drama, horror or anything miserable.
The only thing on television I could tolerate was good, innocent comedy.

I couldn't tolerate being around anyone who held negative talk about themselves or others. I couldn't hold any negative thoughts about myself or others too! I had an intolerance to drama of any kind.

It taught me self-love and love for others, with an understanding of our behaviours.
I slowly but surely learnt about forgiveness, understanding and avoidance of drama. This was just the beginning, however.

~ 40 ~

I began to recognise that my mind needed to heal using only the joyful, comforting and positive aspects of life.

Examples of things that made me feel comfortable were (and still are): gentle comedy; comforting, gentle and positive people; walks in nature; the company of animals; the sunlight; regular drinks of water; good food; exercise; uplifting music; creativity; calm and comforting situations.

I couldn't tolerate any bad news, or challenging situations. The mind was already overflowing with stress, anxiety and depression, so it could only digest comforting and healing surroundings.

It was interesting that the mind was telling me what it needed in order to heal. I followed the "nature of me" at the time.

I know for a fact that what we take in, in form of watching, doing, hearing and surrounding ourselves in has the biggest impact on our minds and bodies.
It is important for us to be selective and respectful to ourselves - to love and care for our minds and bodies.

I have noticed that negative entertainment is extremely addictive to most people, and easy to get soaked up in without even realising that this is occurring.

The benchmark for negativity or shocking television has increased to such extreme levels, as this appears to be the direction in the current trends. Entertainment creators can see the trends and create more of the same, as for them - addiction is good! Television can become a "literal" programme for the mind, absorbing what has been fed to you. The mainstream media tells you what they want you to hear. Extreme money-makers are all feeding one another by programming the minds of many. Just think about how you can repeat the music/jingles or words from big advertisements. Words and music together can stick in the mind and be a huge influence. Choose your own words and music. I no longer buy into controlling addictions, fear-mongering or negative hype from influential media.

The popular books to read appear to be the murder-mystery types, crime thrillers, or war and violence. People are currently flocking to read books of the crime genre and psychological thrillers. One website literally stated that people are addicted to the "darker side of life."
This is sad... and is also reflective.
I remember seeking a happy or uplifting book at one point but couldn't find anything of the sort at that particular time!

Violent games are influencing young people's minds, to the point that they see violence as "normal." We can all see the effects of these.

Music with negative words is like affirmations with musical tones to enhance the words. If you listen to songs with negative words, then your mind will be listening, and sometimes you'll be replaying them over and over in your head! This is another form of programming!

If we are in the company of people who grumble constantly, then we are likely to take in their grumbles in some shape or form, and in many cases, become a grumbly person just the same! I'm not saying to avoid negative people, as they need helpful influences around them, but it would be better to surround yourself more-so with positive and joyous characters so that we can feed the happy wolf with higher quantities and help those who may benefit from our happier outlook. If we feed the happy wolf and inspire others to have a better outlook on life, then we are helping without *controlling*.

It is wonderful to be a happy and positive influence, serving others in a natural way.   When we help others, it helps us to *feel* good.

I love music, television and entertainment just the same as everyone else, but I am now **mindful** of what I choose to take into my mind!   I am also in control of the amount of *time* I *allow* for the digestion of this entertainment.

~ 43 ~

Although we are advanced and have evolved immensely, we are still part of this Earthly nature. This means that our brains will take in any form of "danger", "sadness", "horror", "disaster" etc., whether it hits our brain from what we watch, or hear, sense, smell or taste.

So, I do need to state again that it is beneficial to feed to the "good wolf."

It is also good to escape these entertainment forms by taking a good walk in nature and allowing times of mindfulness. Nature makes us feel good because we are actually *nature*! Switching off our conscious thoughts and entertainments allow a natural flow to the subconscious, so that we can feel our energy and connect to all that is! It also brings a regular opportunity for calm.

Most of us do not allow our minds to drift, as the distractions of our gadgets keep the mind busy. I feel that this has been a gradual development of mental health disorders of today.

Social media can be good and bad, but it is also the chicken's-way-out to hurtful bullying or criticism.

I hope in time that social media will be a gradual build-up to bringing us closer together as *one*.

Using Logic to Heal

Logic is a powerful tool to have. It serves well in what we have gathered in wisdom. This comes with time and experience in life.

One example was that during *my* hardest times, I couldn't *feel* the smile, but I created a smile on my face knowing that one day I would genuinely smile as a happy response to something.

"They" say that smiling sends good chemicals to the brain! Smiling at others generates more smiles, giving other people good chemicals, so, I say "spread the love!"

Today I have genuine laughter and smiles!
It is an amazing act to practice if you need to work on your happiness.

With logic, I knew that exercise was good and healthy to do too. I was worried about my hard, racing heart, but was told that my heart was healthy. I took on that belief and acted upon it by beginning with exercise. I didn't want to exercise at the time, but I felt that it was the right thing to do, to fill my mind with good hormones and chemicals. Science proves the positive effects of exercise with mental health.

At the beginning, I couldn't *feel* the effects of it, but I knew that one day I would, and that it would benefit me in the long run ("long run" – what a pun!).

Today I have great fitness and health!

~ 45 ~

During the most difficult time, I couldn't control my emotions. Fear was overpowering, but I felt and knew that it would help in the long run to practice daily affirmations, good self-talk, and happy belief practices. Today I have a calm and happy mind set.

Logic is an especially useful gift to have. If you know something isn't right, then you can understand through "built logic."

By having experiences in life, we build wisdom. If we have enough time behind us, then we know the differences between what seems right or wrong for us. We have clues on how we can help ourselves or others.

Other people's built logic can also aid *us,* and *their* wisdom can be extremely helpful.

We are here to help one another with our experiences.

It is hard to work on ourselves, particularly when we feel trapped, or exhausted, but trust me it is extremely useful and healing to take time out to work on yourself. The amazing knowledge that we can heal from *anything* if we choose to, is the biggest piece of logic we can have.

The mind is an extremely powerful tool if used with the "good" thoughts and feelings!

Gratitude

Gratitude is a **secret** remedy!

My gratitude began when I thought I was dying!
When I *thought* I had a second chance to live, I slowly but surely rose up!
From that moment onward, I appreciated every rain drop on my face, every movement I could make, every piece of food I could taste, or drink I could swallow. I was even grateful for every bowel movement!
I appreciated those who were (and are) around me, who love me.
I became grateful for every function of my body, and every function of this Earth for supporting my body! We all need oxygen, water and food!   Mother Earth needs more gratitude!

Gratitude is an enormously important subject. This is discussed plentiful in discussions over general happiness, or indeed when wishing to manifest what we choose in life.

Gratitude is a superpower!
I didn't think gratitude would aid me initially, but it certainly helps as a good platform for things. Gratitude brings you back to the **present** time and brings some levels of comfort or excitement for what you currently have.

This may sound harsh, but if you aren't grateful for what you have right this moment, then just take a look at the sufferings of millions on this planet.

I am so grateful for fresh water; food for multiple meals; good health; warmth and comforts. If you have your basic foundations, then you can focus on creating your life in any which means you choose.

I am also extremely grateful for the knowledge that we can truly heal ourselves!

Do you ever think about the amazement of our ability to heal from a cut, or a nasty illness?

Even if an illness takes a few months to heal from, you can truly heal if **you choose** to!

It helps *you* to see what "good" *you* have.

If you haven't already practiced the action of gratitude, then it is a great starting point for happiness in this very moment.

It is amazing to focus on what we **already have** and not to focus on what we *haven't* got.

Only positive, *present* words are amazingly effective. Those words such as I am...; I have...; I can... – are positive and can help you stay in the positive-present.

Avoid words such as: I haven't; I don't; I can't; I mustn't.

An "I can" attitude is already a huge asset to a positive life.

If you feel gratitude for everything and everyone, then happiness is already on its way.

Don't compare yourself to others.
It is good however, to find *inspiration* from others.
There is a difference.

I am happy knowing that I am inspiring others by writing and
leading by good example. It is good for me and equally good
for others.
We *all* have our own satisfactions and challenges. One
person may have all of the money in the world yet be
unhappy rattling around in their huge home.
A child may have all of the latest gadgets and clothing yet
have parents that are never there for them.
Another may appear to have the best body and an amazing
relationship, but behind closed doors have the most raging
arguments or hatred for themselves and others.
Someone may live in one of the most beautiful resorts in the
world yet lack internal happiness.
Someone may have the biggest smile always yet be disguising
their biggest frown.
Everything isn't always as it appears to be.
I'm sure you get my drift!

It is also important not to worry about who/what you can
lose! Focus on all of the wonderful people and things you
have right this minute.
Do not feel *guilt* for what you have either, as *guilt* is not a
comfortable or good feeling. We were all born into
situations that are different to others and we all make our
choices based on so many factors.

Always trust in your own decisions.

Some people complain about their lives being so busy and stressful, but it is *their* creation of *their* lives. Once we are aware of the fact that it is our responsibility to take care of our own minds and choices, then it holds great power in our lives overall. Don't look to blame others.

I have a great example of someone I know, who blames a teacher from his childhood for his lack of confidence. The teacher bullied and criticised him frequently.
This obviously isn't nice for a child, but once you're aware of your own mastery, you can change anything about your mind, therefore every situation in your life.
We can clean up our previous perceptions and begin to believe in ourselves, making life work *for* us!

Be happy, be free!

Every morning I deliberately think about what I am grateful for! I began writing these things down on a piece of paper (recycled paper!) and placed it next to my bed. I had the intention to pick this up first, instead of my previous habit of picking up the mobile phone!

You can write down what you are grateful for every day and have it handy to pick up just as soon as you wake. It literally takes a minute or two and is much healthier for your mind than allowing your mobile phone to take precedence over your mental health.

Please don't see the list as exhaustive or limited. You can amend it as often as you like!

This is my example (not in any order of priority): -

- I am grateful to wake up today!
- I am grateful to have slept!
- I am grateful to have a healthy, functioning brain.
- I am grateful to have a healthy, functional body.
- I am grateful to have food, water and shelter.
- I am grateful to have work that pays.
- I am grateful to have loved ones around me.
- I am grateful to have a vehicle for travel.
- I am grateful for an abundance of clothing.
- I am grateful for my natural abilities!

You can look at gratitude in specific areas of life too.

Let us take the specific area of "the relationship with my partner."

This is taking the good points of a partner in life, which could even help your relationship with them!

Here are some examples: -

- I am grateful that my partner understands who I am.
- I am grateful for my partner's loyalty.
- I am grateful that my partner is so kind.

- I am so grateful that my partner helps me to laugh.

This doesn't have-to be so rigid either. There are relaxed ways to express the gratitude. The trick is to recognise the greatness you have right in this moment, to live in the present with such gratitude.

With "relationships," this could simply be the relationship you have with yourself!
You could raise points such as: -

- I am so grateful to have found my happiness.
- I am so grateful that I love my own company.
- I am so grateful for my fantastic personality and easy-going mind.
- I am so grateful for my gifts and abilities.

This is also an act of self-love, which is good!

Obviously, it isn't necessarily using such static thoughts or words. Just the recognition of things gives the same great feeling. An example I can give is: "Wow, my house is just perfect as it is," or, "I love my car. It drives so well and has been loyal transport."

Gratitude is the recognition of what and who we have NOW, and just feeling how wonderful it is.
In fact, the brain understands things better when we focus on the "NOW" – on the present situation that we have.

The present is a gift! A gift is a present!

When I think about what and who I am grateful for, I also feel
the excitement of this. These things may not seem a lot to
you or me, but there are too many people on this planet who
don't have anything or anyone other than their own survival!
So be grateful and excited about everything and everyone in
your life in this present moment.
Sometimes if we experience a lack of something in life it
brings more gratitude for *that*!

If you believe in the ability to manifest, then this is a great
tool to bring in **more** of who and what you are grateful for. It
is a strong magnetic force of positivity.
Be aware of your *specific* words as well. The mind will listen
with every detail! Only be grateful for who and what you
truly wish for. Everyone is obviously extremely individual!

If you know that we are made up of billions of individually-
intelligent-cells and that we are not as solid as we experience
with our limited senses, then you will know that these cells
vibrate at a particular frequency. We attract what we put
out due to everything being "energy." Our thoughts are
intelligently alive and attract the same.

We attract with "thought, word and deed."
The Secret; The Law of Attraction; Universal Laws and the Bibles all say the same thing...
"Ask, believe, receive."
"Ask and yea shall receive." "What you put out; you get back."
You can also ask for help. There are many conscious beings that are here to aid us.

We create with everything we think, say and do. Add passion and belief and it will come to you in a great force.
I healed myself by thinking, speaking, acting and believing myself better! It is the genuine truth of life. Already, this is all you need to know. This book simply goes into detail for a better understanding.
I believe that we never die in our energy form, we just manifest into different forms with our consciousness. We interconnect with all life forms and their consciousnesses!
If we live in the present moment, we can see that every day and every second is an opportunity for any change we choose to make.
We are given the law of choice. There is a universal law that is strictly in place, given by the greatest source of all life that states we were all given the law of choice.
In every situation, I aim for love, peace and joy.
This beautiful Earth has been created in order to play with this magic, as an amazing simulation of physical reality, coupled with our entirety.
Free your mind and live the best possibilities!

Positive Belief in Yourself

Please love and respect yourself. It is the most important thing you can do for your own mind. Just a reminder that: - **You are the master of your own mind and that it is *your* job!**

*Do not let it be the *job* of other **people's opinions**!
*Do not allow it to be the *job* of **the media**!

The media includes: -

The television!
The cinema!
The news!
Advertisements!
Newspapers!
Magazines!
Game consoles!

Be in control of any deliberate sources of influences on the mind. Only take the positive influences that encourage a sense of comfort and happiness to you. This involves listening to your natural instincts!

If you know it is *your* job to keep *you* happy and contented, but you don't know where to begin, then firstly be **aware** of how to speak to yourself (with thought and word) and how you *allow* others to speak to you. Are your own words and thoughts loving, respectful and comforting for *you*?

Are your words to others with the underlying intention of
love, respect and comfort?
Did you know that what we send out reflects back on us?
In the past I've felt the discomfort by criticising or agreeing to
someone's criticism. If you love yourself and others for the
amazing *beings* that we are, then you would find it
exceedingly difficult to speak adversely about yourself and
others.

Learn to love yourself first and then learn to love others,
unconditionally!

When other people criticise us, it is only a reflection of their
own insecurities. It is also a lesser understanding and lesser
level of respect for individual choice and uniqueness. We all
have our sense of "self." If you love and respect yourself
enough to be your true self, then it doesn't matter what
others think of you. People will always hold their own
perceptions of themselves and others anyway! It takes a
unique and *true* character to create the greatest version of
you! Be proud to be who you uniquely are.
If you are brave enough to be who you truly are and hold
confidence about yourself, then it does not matter what
other people think.

Be loving and respectful to your mind, with words and
thoughts of your own choice.

Work on your inner world and it will also create your outer world! The development of "the self" has so many personal benefits.

Imagine you are a happier, more confident person. It would bring about better life experiences; more people will be excited to be with you and it will help inspire others.

Our thoughts and actions create our beliefs and in turn shape our reality!

Imagine two people with the same **foundation** of mind-set. They've both chosen their own set of beliefs over several adult years.

Now imagine the difference between the one who believes they are weak and frightened of everything and compare that to someone who believes they are courageous and strong. Who do you think has the greatest life experience? One will be trapped in their own prison, while the other is fulfilling their dreams!

You have all been given the gift of free will! You create your own reality!

I'm sure many of you will know this *secret* by now:
People who feel happy and successful in their own lives are those who have not given up at the first hurdle or been afraid of failure. Those who have continued to try and try again haven't always exposed their failures, as respect themselves so much so that they focus on the positive outcomes.

~ 57 ~

There are many quotes referring to "picking yourself up every time you fall." When we were children, we may have fallen and grazed our knees, only to get upset a little before getting back up to follow the next adventure. Hopefully, for most of us, a little graze didn't stop us from having fun. We learn about what works and what doesn't.
Think like the child... always discovering and learning... always finding the fun in everything... looking for the next adventure ... and picking yourself up every time you fall! Be brave enough to brush yourself off and try again. Life isn't about staying down. There is no failure! There is only an experience for personal growth!

We are all learning and growing. Just the other day I was feeling nervous about a challenge I was expecting at work, followed by a new teaching session I was going to be leading. I felt the need to have someone comfort me before these events. It seemed that I was looking for emotional support. As a natural "analyser" of things, I wanted to know why I needed the comfort of another for something only *I* can deal with. In life we can either deal with things or hide away from things. Hiding isn't allowing personal growth. I realised that I needed to practice what I preach, by telling myself that it is all about confidence in my own ability and simply believing in myself. I questioned the difference between having someone there to comfort me, or having my own mind bring comfort. It is so easy for others to say, "You'll be alright." Why do others have more confidence in us than we do in ourselves at times? They know that we can handle something. So, questioning my own mind, I realised that it didn't actually matter if someone else echoed the same words that I was thinking (from knowing what to say to myself). I remembered that if we think we are going to fail and at the same time have a mind-set of failure and disaster, then this is negative forecasting and bringing a lack of confidence to the table.

If we *believe* it will be successful and give it everything we can, with an "I can..." attitude, then we can positively forecast with a positive, forecasted outcome.

It is comforting the mind and taking positive action.

In the end, having faith in myself and looking at solutions, I had a very successful set of events.

Another way of thinking is knowing that - **to live this life, we need to literally live-our-lives without worrying about the opinions of others.** To know that you are amazing in your uniqueness and for that reason alone, allow yourself to shine! Think of well-known artists - whether painters, sketchers, writers, knitters, singers, actors... When you think about these creative people who have allowed their natural and unique talents to shine, they have portrayed themselves well in the world!

It is better to try with all of your might and with belief in yourself, than not to try at all.

Despite our so called "failures," I believe that these are benchmarks that we can use for benchmarks of improvement, like using criticism as feedback. All feedback from others or ourselves is positive feedback, for however we wish to use it. There is actually no failure, just simply *experience*. It is up to us if we wish to get up after a fall or stay down. Would you stay down after a fall? Usually you wouldn't, so why would you stay down after a loss? Keep reaching for the stars!

Images with Words

As you have probably gathered so far – words are enormously powerful. I have said many times that words can create wars or deliver peace.

Thought and word manifests our own reality. Thoughts and words are a very real energy!

One person alone can change any of their situations with a simple decision, even if it is changing their own perception of a circumstance.

A group of people with collective, focussed thoughts or words can make immense changes.

We can collectively change our reality and therefore our future.

Just look at influential figures that have come and gone in our world. Their words of "power" have influenced millions of people.

We can controversially say that some leaders have influenced many in a negative sense. I'm sure we can all think of at least one! Then, we can see that there are some leaders that have *positively* influenced many millions!

The mind is immensely powerful and will listen to every word you say to yourself. If you believe something is good, then your mind will believe it is. You can lie to yourself, and it becomes the truth.

In order to add strength to words, you can add an image for a particular association. Can you recall a song with inspirational words that has been associated with a movie that you've seen? Say for example the Rocky movies (if you don't mind). The music during the uprising moments can feel very inspiring. If you place that music on during a personal workout, you can be driven to believe that you are "uprising" and getting stronger. Can you see that association?

More simply, if you visualise yourself as an extraordinarily strong person and tell yourself you are extraordinarily strong, the images coupled with the words make the belief immensely powerful. It brings a **feeling** that associates with that. That feeling can bring about a greater sense of "power."

Your mind will most certainly listen to that combination of thought, imagery and feeling to bring about this belief. Remember the effects of your senses?   Music for your ears; Images for your eyes; Smells for your nose...   These senses can empower your thoughts when brought together positively.

Place pictures and inspirational music with your words for the association in order to give more power to the *words*. If you tell yourself that you are confident and *see* yourself as confident too, then how would you *look* if you were confident? How would you *feel* with the words, uplifting music and image of yourself?

Believe you are *that* version of yourself! Really feel it! Adding the strength of **passion** will enhance your belief and make it immensely powerful.

~ 62 ~

With the positive picture that you paint, along with the music (perhaps even a nice smell!) and the words you choose - will create the amazing **feeling**. The feeling of **joy** and **excitement** is enormously powerful for your mind, body and energy.

Now just add the power of belief! If you can master this, then you could even attempt to *add* an enhanced, amazing feeling!

Your mind will create who and what you believe you are. Try these statements below and paint a picture of how this looks, and then *feel* the passion, excitement and joy! -

"I am amazing!"

"I am a powerful being!"

"I am an amazing gift!"

"I am beautiful!"

"I can do anything I set my mind to."

"I am so rich in love and joy."

"I am so full of happiness."

"I am full of drive and passion."

"My mind and body is extremely healthy and powerful."

"I trust and depend on my own choices."

"I am calm."

"I have an amazing memory."

"My body knows how to use my food and drink effectively for amazing wellbeing."

"I can do anything!"

"I am..."

"I can..."
And most importantly: -
"I love myself!"

If you can begin to practice this in front of the mirror with the associated expressions, then the enhancement is intense.
Smile... believe... receive.
Make the statement... believe... receive.

Always attempt to have a clear picture so that your mind knows.

Put a picture with each statement that empowers your words and feel that joy or excitement! This is powerful work.

I know some of you reading this will say things like, "but it's not true." Well, let me tell you that anything you *choose* to be true is actually true! Not only that, but every single one of us on this planet is beautiful; amazing; a gift; and can do anything we choose. Be the positive, loving, comforting master of your mind and get the best out of this life experience.
Now, go back to the statements and believe that they are true!
With any statement you tell yourself with such powerful imagery and positive feeling, coupled with the power of the present moment, your mind will accept it completely.
If you *choose* to be happy, then you are!

The trick is to keep working on your mind and to be repetitive, daily!
If you don't believe it or feel it today, then keep doing it for a few weeks with the pictures and images together until you really feel it! When you notice the difference within yourself, you will begin to believe what "*I*" am saying!
Persistence and Patience is key, never giving up on hurdles!
Any backward movement, just simply tell yourself it may be one step back, but you're moving two steps forward!
Always keep the power of positivity and the present!

It is like physical exercise, the amazing results come in time, so it is worth the effort you put in.
Once you feel the excitement or joy together with the words and images, then you will create such amazing and powerful feelings that make you feel so much happier.

Make your choices on **how** you wish to be, then be that person! Don't be a carbon copy! Be your unique and true self. Work on who you truly are. Be truthful to yourself, and powerful all of the way!
If people love you, then they wish to see you happy, calm, contented and confident.
This is **your** life!
You are your own master!
Some people need to fit in with some form of identity, but I feel that if you love yourself unconditionally, then it doesn't matter what labels people put on you, or how you have

previously seen yourself. Love who you are and then you don't depend on the labels that are easily dished out.
I used to find confidence from being in great shape until I went through my "transformational time." I had-to learn unconditional love for myself, which taught me to understand that it is who we truly are that is important, not what we do or how we look. We can be in great shape yet still be unhappy inside. I noticed that we are still *who* we are whether we are skinny, fat, unhealthy or healthy.

In order to love yourself whole heartedly, then I truly believe that it is vital to have pure, unconditional love for yourself no matter how you look.

Choosing Your Intentions for the Day

When you wake with **gratitude**, then it is great to keep the momentum going!

I like to choose *how* my day will go!

This is also enormously powerful, as it is working on the present and creating an intended feeling for the day.

We can all do this, even if we are in a pickle with any mood, or ongoing mental health struggles.

If you don't initially *feel* the decisions when you think, or read out particular choices or intentions, then that is okay!

Again, it is about daily practice and persistence until you do feel it!

If you truly wish to find happiness in your life, then the efforts of daily persistence will pay off! I am speaking with truth of experience.

If you struggle, then remind yourself that you are a true warrior and a great fighter of love, peace and positivity.

A set of intentions can be extremely simple, such as this example: -

"Today I choose to be happy and calm. It will be enjoyable and how *I* intend it to be, with happiness! I shall only accept *loving* and *joyous* energy to impact me *positively*."

Believe what you intend and feel positive power behind it, along with some great images of how you set yourself to be!

Just add a daily intention (or several - it's up to you!), to your list of things that you are grateful for. Your own set of "gratitude" and "intention" needs to be truest to your **own** desires!

As mentioned, gratitude and intention can be extremely simple, but I am someone who likes a bit more detail and power-provoking words.

Here is an elaborate set of daily intentions: -

"Today, I intend to see what and who **"I"** intend to see, with happiness, joy and peace!"

"Today I promise I shall love and approve of myself, with the knowledge that I am beautiful and unique."

"Today I shall remember that I love and trust myself with every choice I make, with every step of the day being exactly what **"I"** wish to experience."

"I intend to move forward with my own choices and no resistance to life."

"I intend to have a fantastic day, with a happy mood that nobody can affect. I am protected and safe in my own energy."

"I choose to help anyone who needs my help, with the greatest intention of overall good and the protection of my own happiness."

This is similar to my morning practices in order to set my mind for the day. Our minds are enormously powerful, and our thoughts create our feelings, therefore our energy! Our energy will attract more of the same energy.

If you do believe in energy and that we attract more of what we think, feel, say and do, coupled with who we surround ourselves with, then you may know that we are like huge magnets to the universe. Be mindful of what and who you would like to attract to your life. As the saying goes, "Be careful of what you wish for."

Wise Guidance

Another Secret Revealed: **You are the one who decides *how* you respond to *anything* in life.**
It is all about wisdom and perception.
Everything begins with a neutral response.
As a baby we love everything about ourselves. Everything is new and investigatory! There is excitement and joy for everything we experience.
We naturally cried when we had a discomfort or a need, which is a clever communication method for the mother to calculate.

In time we are conditioned into how we should behave and respond to everything.

It is time to forget the conditioning and to begin to bring in your own perception and response to things.

If you have been fortunate enough to have people inspire and guide you in your life, then you will already have a head-start in *knowing* some/all **comforting thoughts for many situations**. With wise guidance, let me help you find your bespoke…: -

"Comforting thoughts for every situation."

People who have guided or inspired us come from all walks of life. They can essentially be our parents/grandparents; our work colleagues; our schoolteacher/s; our friends; a therapist; sibling; a sport's personality; an author! etc.

No matter *who* this may be for you, or however you wish to work this next process - it is a useful set of skills to have in your mind!

We have all developed belief systems over the period of our lives with influences, observations and experiences.

This is the process, but the actual **words** that **comfort *you*** may be different to what **comforts *me***: -

Imagine the wisest, most comforting set of people (I.E the most perfect set of parents/grandparents/any role model of your wisest choice). If you don't know anyone wise, or comforting enough, then *imagine* the wisest, most comforting person.

No human being is perfect, so if you prefer to use your "imagined" wise person or even someone beyond our *physical* realm then please do!

Obviously, you can imagine anyone's personal advice during any event in your life, but if you could imagine the wise words that would be said when you need them, at any time, as if they are talking to you in your mind, then this is an especially useful and comforting tool. I like to describe it as going through the brain's file of words in order to find a set that would comfort you.

Obviously, please *literally* speak to people about any concern or challenge you have, as it certainly is fantastic and always advisable to talk. In fact, I urge you always to discuss any problems with friends, colleagues, family or those that you trust. As mentioned before, we all hold our logic and wisdom built from experiences, so something new to us is old to someone else. Just remember how you felt as a kid going through something that appeared to be tragic, but as an adult would be trivial.

This method is just a *response* to a "situation," or a "negative thought" during any situation, which can help your own mind effectively.

The most important mind-set for *any* challenging time is to focus on the SOLUTION and not the PROBLEM. Of course, we need to know the problem in order to calculate a solution, just the same as understanding the discomfort in order to find a means of comfort; as well as knowing what is negative to understand the positive.

It's all about "having a word with yourself," but listening to your feelings whilst doing this.
When you feel fear, anger, jealousy, hatred, disgust (whatever you feel is uncomfortable within you at any given time), then it is all about having a word with yourself, using comforting thoughts and words in order to feel comfortable again!

When you have a word with yourself and you feel happier, stronger, better, comfortable... then it is the correct set of words for you. If you have words with yourself and you feel unhappy, sad, or have any uncomfortable feeling or emotion, then you know these are not the right set of words for you, unless (unusually) you prefer to feel uncomfortable!
In other words (sorry about the pun), it's about finding a healthy perception.

Let me give you an example.
I was once angry with my neighbours for playing their music too loud on a regular basis. I thought about a possible **solution** and knew that I needed to ask them nicely to turn their music down, which I did. They did turn their music down, fortunately, but I was left with that anger inside of me. I needed to have a "word with myself."
It was important for me to tell myself that **anger is only harming "me" and that my neighbours are not worth my health!** I am the master of my own mind!
I also told myself that the music wasn't actually harming me either. The bonus was that they kindly acknowledged their error and corrected it.
I finally told myself to release the problem from my mind, as I had resolved it with a solution!

People also think that a rainy day is a bad, dreary day. If you have ever stayed in a hot, dry country, you will know that rain is very much a gift. Rain gives us life, as it supplies for plants, which is obviously our food!

~ 73 ~

A sunny day is just as beautiful as a rainy day. Every day is beautiful and holds magic!   Can you see the benefit of that perception?

Another example can be "Tinnitus." I have had tinnitus for many years. You can allow it to be your enemy, or you can make friends with it. If you constantly battle with your own mind it brings such discomfort and potentially, depression. I have learnt to ignore it and place it to the back of my mind. I am only aware of it when I think about it, but what is there to think about? That's the ultimate question. The answer is that if there is no cure, then just to ignore it. Learn to live with it!

I have the perception of the benefit of beautiful visualisations, coupled with intentions.
Sometimes I take deep breaths inwardly and allow a golden colour to fill my body and mind, visually. I then release the breath with any selective colour that *I* can visualise as negative, such as grey or black.

Perception is perhaps another word for "belief."
Our thoughts and words that interact with one another are very powerful. Take in the thoughts and words that *you* choose in order to have a healthy perception for yourself!

Thoughts and words are always heard by your mind, energy and body. They are also a command to the universe. What you think and say to yourself and to others will always land

~ 74 ~

up in your own mind and energy. It reflects out into the universe and always comes back to you. This is wonderfully magical if you think about it with positive perception!

You know yourself that when you've taken on the words of others, they can make you feel a particular way, so only allow the positive opinions of others to impact you well! People can see when you respect yourself enough only to accept positive or comforting opinions. So, please respect yourself by respecting your mind and body. If you hear the opinions of others that you don't wish to hear, you can simply ignore the opinions, or use a diplomatic response.

Sometimes people don't realise that their words are being harmful.

Before I went through my mental health "transformation," a friend of mine once had a habit of calling me a "dumbass" when I was trying to bring humour to conversations. I stopped trying to be funny as a result, but I realised I was jeopardising my own happy character. They wondered why I was being too serious. I had to explain gently that I didn't like being called a dumbass, as it felt disrespectful, and I was only trying to bring joy. She explained that she preferred it when I was happy and that she thought her comment was just her way of attempting humour.

When we understand each other more for our actions, it helps our relationships.

It isn't selfish to be kind and loving to yourself. It is vital!

So initially, here are the most important set of *directions* to remember! :-

Be the kindest person to yourself!
Be gentle with yourself!
Respect yourself!
You are your own best friend!
Be at peace with yourself!
Love yourself!
Master your own mind to benefit *you*!
You are just as worthy as everyone else!
Learn to understand yourself so that you can forgive yourself.

At the end of the day, you are the one who has-to live with yourself!
You are worth working on!
It is extremely beneficial to master your mind.
This life is a gift that *you* chose to have!
Be responsible for your choices in order to create the best life for yourself!
Going back to the subject of placing your wisest, most comforting person into your mind to give you the most comforting words for every situation - I want to give you some more examples of this.
For me, I mostly know what I need to hear, so I am literally telling myself what I need to hear (or know) in order to feel better.
I literally go through the filing cabinet in my mind to find thoughts that make a situation more comfortable. I can

sometimes go through different sets of thoughts, still feeling uncomfortable, until I find the type of thought that suddenly brings a sense of ease in my mind and body.

I once felt nervous about a friend who was diagnosed with cancer. I had-to find my own coping mechanism in order to be useful to them. Obviously, I would understand that their mind would be severely challenged, so needed to think of helpful words for them too! I just wanted to be strong for *them*.

I went through a category of thoughts that I thought might help, but I struggled. It's important to keep working through helpful thoughts though. I stumbled upon one thought which didn't seem genuinely nice to think, but it gave me instant calm! Nobody needs to know what thoughts comfort you!

I don't mind sharing my pattern of thoughts that aided me in this situation. I think it's important to be calm and rational for people who are going through tough challenges, as they don't want to see that they upset loved ones around them. So, with this, I tried each thought to see which one made me feel the calmest.

Here are some of them: -

"It is their path for their choice of growth here on Earth."

"I can only send them Reiki and be there physically when they wish to have my company."

"We are not physically attached. I do love them however."

~ 77 ~

"She's under the health professional's care."
"I have no control over other people's choices, or health... So, I have to know that there is nothing I can do other than to help them practically."

It is true that we all create our own paths and make our own decisions in life.
My personal belief is that before we are born, we have pre-decided which experiences we wish to have; which parents we need for these experiences; the friends and enemies, or guides (human or animal!) that we need during each chapter of our lives. I believe that we come from a *home* of another frequency of energy and that we return to that once our physical bodies expire. During our time in *that* home, we are calculating what experiences we choose next for the continual evolving of ourselves.
Contradictory to this, I also believe that we create whatever we choose to create during our stay here, as Earthlings!
The power of thought, word, action, passion and belief can create an amazing set of circumstances, whether negative or positive. It all depends which mind-set you choose. The thoughts, words, actions and beliefs create a feeling that picks up the frequency which attracts the same level of energy.
The amazing thing to know is that the Universe works *for* you! So, you give out what you want to receive!

Here are some other situations that I have attached thoughts to in order to aid myself (a lot of these stem from personal beliefs, so they may not be for everyone! I am simply giving helpful examples).: -

Challenging work situations:

"It's just work."

"It's only human created."

"I can only work at the speed I am comfortable and effective with for good quality, so I am taking one step at a time. I'd rather do that than rush and make mistakes that will come back on me."

"I'm prioritising my work-load in order of importance and using my time-management skills. It promotes the best possible outcome."

"What I don't finish today will have to wait until tomorrow."

Times of Anger:

"Anger only harms the self. It was my choice to respond with anger, so I shall choose to allow peace within myself."

"They don't deserve my health, so I allow my anger to go."

"I shall breathe in love and breathe out anger." - Requiring that action.

General anxiety flare-ups:

"This is just anxiety."

"I am safe."

"I am okay."

"This will pass."

"Breathe gently into the nose, down to the lower core, hold it and then slowly release through the mouth."

"Breathe in "Calm."

Anxiety of Something in Particular:

"This is an opportunity to understand something about myself. This will help me calculate what I want and what I don't want, by linking up the cause of how I can help myself."

"If I face this fear, I can increase my level of bravery!"

"Little baby steps for a huge step overall."

Illness:

"This is temporary, it will pass." Or "I'm getting better every day in every way."

"An illness does not own me. I can heal, as this is only temporary."

"I am strong enough!"

Big changes:

"I can adapt to change, as it is the one thing guaranteed in life. It will help me to grow as a person. See it as an opportunity."

"This is exciting!"

"When one door closes, another one opens."

Disagreements:

"Everyone believes their perception is right, so allow them. We have no control over others. Let it be."

"Agree to disagree."

People need healing:

"I will work as an inspirer somehow."

Moving to A New House:

"This is a new chapter with a new canvas to paint. I shall build new memories. I chose to move. A home can be anywhere so long as it brings shelter and the necessities I need."

"This is exciting!"

"This is meant to be."

This is hard:

"This is an opportunity to evolve and grow. I can figure out a resolve for this with just one comforting thought."

Passing-over of a Loved One:

"I can see that this is the end of their experience as that particular character, and a time to celebrate their experiences on Earth. They have gone back home to perfection. I may miss them here, but they celebrate the reunion of their rebirth back home, so I shall try to be happy for them."

Bad Mental Health Day:

"I may have gone a step backwards, but I am healing, so this shall pass, and I shall be moving forwards by two steps!"
"I am safe and well."
"This too shall pass."

Self-Doubt:

"I can do this."
"I've done this before."
"I am amazing."
"I shall face this with great strength."

An Event:

"See it as exciting!"
"This is an adventure."

These are just some examples that spring to mind, but it does help to know that all challenges are actually *opportunities*. As we go through experiences, it helps us to grow and evolve. The greater the challenge, the greater the growth. Where there is a "challenge," it is extremely beneficial to focus on a particular solution. There is a solution for mind health in terms of gathering the right perspective; Then there is the power of change, by recognising that you can change *anything* in life, if you choose to!

If you can see happiness on the other side of something then it is worth facing the fear.

Small or large amendments can change a person's life so much, i.e. Being aware of and amending thought patterns; getting appropriate therapy; changing simple habits for better health; moving home; divorcing; changing careers; putting your faith into something or someone; letting go; acquiring knowledge, and so forth.

It is important to always move forward. If you had thousands of pounds in your bank account and you lost about twenty pounds, would you focus on that twenty pound loss for the rest of your life? Or would you remember the thousands of pounds?

If you could view the thousands of pounds as a comparison to happiness, then you wouldn't lose your happiness over one event if you still have the potential to have an abundance of happiness. So don't allow one thing in life to ruin your entire level of happiness. Move forward!

Although we choose our thoughts, words and actions, it is nice to trust life with the flow we choose. A bit like sitting in a canoe and allowing a river's current to carry you along your journey (just relaxing into the flow). You may catch the odd rock along the journey, but you can continue on, trusting in the canoe, carrying you through this journey. In other words, just trust in life and the natural flow and guidance. We have got *choices* all of the way through life however, which can take us down different avenues and bring us different views and experiences.

If things get a bit tough, we have the power to step back and see things as the observer. It sometimes helps me to see from an observer's perspective, knowing we are here for the experiences. It also helps to see things from a neutral, or bird's eye perspective.

Even without situations or circumstances in life, we all have thoughts flying through our minds. It's important to listen to what we are telling ourselves. The little chitter chatter that flies through our minds can be good or bad/comfortable or uncomfortable. It is important to pay attention to how our personal thoughts make us *feel*. If we feel uncomfortable with certain thoughts, then it is useful to have that awareness and just stop that negative thought!
Once I am aware of negative chitter chatter in my mind, I suddenly stop and change it instantly. Sometimes I calculate the resolving thought, but sometimes I simply play some uplifting music and focus my attention on that! It is an extremely valuable tool to be aware of our thoughts. It is particularly important to have awareness of **when** we are likely to hold negative chitter chatter in our minds. I find that I am vulnerable to this type of pattern when I am driving. In some ways the awareness of this is easier, as the radio is right in front of my fingers!

With the words of the *Wolf*, it's much healthier to feed the good wolf. I know personally that I would prefer to have all of the positive aspects of good, comforting and loving thoughts. It is the difference to living in *fear and sadness or* living in *joy* and *love*!

All thoughts contribute immensely to an extraordinarily strong set of beliefs! These are important attributes to ourselves and can influence to our own: -

Confidence
Courage
Freedom
Self-love & love towards others.
Self-image
...Even survival!

These are huge aspects of our lives!

Some of us have naturally allowed the opinions or control of others to impact how we feel about ourselves.
We have allowed the opinion of others to impact our beliefs.
When we are told we are stupid, weak, pathetic, ugly, dramatic, useless (so many other hurtful criticisms), it can feed our thoughts and become stored in our subconscious.
We then end up *believing* and *behaving* in that particular way. From this negative method, people grow to believe they have no place in society or lack self-esteem or

confidence.   Their mind can become a prison of such continual negative thoughts. The good news is that our thoughts can be re-programmed!

If you are reading this book, then let me tell you that you are strong enough to set yourself free and understand your value in this life!

Although it is extremely easy for me to say – the most important thing is **not** to allow other people's opinions to form your own belief or opinion of yourself. Never allow anyone to insult your intelligence or disrespect you.

You are who you *choose* to be. You are as amazing as you decide to be!

Have you ever seen the image of a small cat looking at him/herself in a mirror, only to see a big cat such as a Tiger or Lion looking back? We truly are who and what we believe we are. Stand by the set of beliefs *you* choose to have of yourself.

Remember that when people criticise or speak to someone in a detrimental way, it's usually a reflection of their own insecurities or frustrations.

The other thing to remember is that beauty is in the eye of the beholder and that "one man's rubbish is another man's treasure" (as the saying goes). These are all relevant statements, as we all have our own view and perceptions of things and people!

Let your own mind rule yourself! You are the master of your own thoughts! Create yourself as you choose! Be strong enough to be who you truly are. Have enough respect for yourself... for the *real* you to shine through!

So, ask yourself, who do you want to be? Who are you *really*? Who are you without all of the *masks* or expectations of others?

Love yourself for who you are. Love the fact that you are unique and extremely beautiful in your own way! Be free to express who you truly are! Let your true self flow!

When you love and respect yourself, you know what you wish to hear, either from others or from yourself. Don't accept anything that isn't of love or respect.

Positive Affirmations

To reprogram your mind with a healthy and gradual, long term method, I totally believe in daily affirmations.

When I needed to find a way of healing from uncontrollable fear and uncontrollable emotions, I gave myself positive words constantly. Even if I didn't have the *feeling* behind it initially, it grew and grew until it was powerful enough to become my reality!
This is like doing daily physiotherapy exercises to an injured limb until you can use it well again. If it's practiced daily, the benefits can be amazing for the long term!

Affirmations are repeated phrases that you say to yourself for personal benefit. They can aid with confidence, calm, joy and anything you choose when it comes to personal preference!
It helps to have poetry attached in order to have the addictive continuation. I couldn't rhyme with many, but the ones that did, were the ones that stuck, which is extremely helpful.
If you choose to make big changes within yourself, then you truly need to keep the affirmations going throughout the day, every day, even if you have set times, such as morning, midday and evening, for twenty times during each session. The affirmations are great to continue until the mind has accepted them as true! You will know by behaviours and feelings!

There are some affirmations for general happiness. These are the ones I began with.: -

"I am getting better every day in every way."
"I am getting calmer and calmer every day."
"I am safe and well. I can do this."
"My body is healing my mind, and my mind is healing my body."
"I am getting happier and happier every day."
"I am young, fit and healthy."

If you want to go for the present tense, which is enormously powerful, then affirmations look like this: -

"I am happy!"
"I am strong!"
"I am calm and confident."
"I am just as vital as everyone else."
"I have the same Universal rights as everyone else."
"I have my equally-important place in this world."

When we say these things to ourselves, it is important to note how we *feel*.

Let us look at how we can change our self-belief now...
So, imagine you know and recognise that you have been put-down for most of your life, or that your confidence is lacking. You too have perhaps added to the negative self-talk of putting yourself down. Firstly, **forgive yourself**, as it truly hasn't been your fault! We are all learning in this game of life. With fresh awareness, know that you can forgive past patterns of self-hate or negative thought-patterns. We had-to be who we had-to be in order to get through circumstances in life. It is now time to forgive yourself.
Give up the blame on other people such as your parents, as they are also only learning, given their experiences and hardships. It is useful to attempt to understand those who we have blamed for our circumstances. Our parents would have been affected by *their* parents and role models. They would have also had methods, struggles and perhaps severities in life. I can see that we are all children trying to take on the big game of life; building experiences and responsibilities we were never qualified for! Even educational or work-place qualifications are human-created!

If you now know that you are the master of your own mind and life, then you can change anything or *everything!* If you now know that *you* are the one who tells you how you feel and what your life choices are, then life can take a strong U-turn!
Absolutely everything was meant to be. Even picking this book up in order to make amazing changes in your life – is meant to be!

~ 89 ~

Just think about those people who have so much self-belief and confidence about themselves. It is amazing how we are attracted to positive, confident, bubbly people. With those positive people, it is hard to view them in a negative way. With that type of behaviour, they are attracting more of the same towards themselves.

Affirmations can be used to create a new set of personal beliefs. Affirmations can be enough, so long as you believe them and you are continual, until you become what you have set for yourself. When you add belief and positive feeling to the affirmations, they become much more powerful. Your subconscious gradually begins to believe and behave in the way in which you are *programming* yourself. You have your choice of words and thoughts, which create the feelings you choose to have! So, choose only those thoughts and words that work **for** you, or even, **serve** you! Don't give yourself over to someone else's beliefs! Watch your internal chitter chatter. **Any negative thoughts need to be stopped and replaced by positive thoughts a few times over!**

So, set your *powerful, emotive* affirmations!

Work out the negative aspects of your life or mind at this moment of time and intend to work on them in order to make your weaknesses your strengths, or to calculate a positive response. Your negative aspects show-up in negative self-talk. Here are some *examples* of calculating the negative or weak aspects you may think exist in your life: -

"I am unhealthy."

"I'm not brave enough."

"I can't do that."

"I am stupid."

"I'm weak."

"I'm not clever enough to do that."

"I can't afford that."

"I'm too old now."

"I'd never be any good at that."

"I could never wear that."

Other negative self-talk can be comments to yourself that continue to give your mind the belief that you're generally not good enough. Comments such as: -

"Ah, that's typical of me."

"I can never get this right."

"That always happens to me."

"Oh, what an idiot."

"Stupid!"

Anything that gives your mind the impression that you simply have no value for yourself.

If you can relate to anything like this, then these ideals may have been programmed for so long, that your subconscious mind believes that you're perhaps not good, or worthy enough to have complete happiness! It is important to believe in the things that will make life work positively for you. Take your mind and master your truths and values. Again, "who do you wish to be?" Or "Who are you _**really**_?"

Simply believe in yourself! Every – Single – One of us, is just as beautiful and valuable!
Love yourself with courage and self-respect! You owe it to yourself!

Just think about the movie, The Wizard of Oz. What great lessons on self-belief that movie has! Remember the Lion who had little courage and continued to believe that? He was told that he had no courage, so believed what he was told.
The Lion eventually proved to himself and the others that he actually *did* have courage. Once he recognised that he *can* be courageous, he began believing and behaving in a courageous way!
The medal that the lion received enhanced his beliefs as a symbol of his courage. Always give yourself encouragement when you are who you truly are, even if it is simply a pat on the back!

We all have the power to face our fears and change our thoughts and behaviours. Our best lives are usually on the other side of fear.

If you wish to become more confident, or positive, or generally happy - then begin by simply being aware of what you are saying to yourself.

~ 92 ~

Awareness is the major key to changing your thoughts. If
you are aware of any negative self-talk, whether in your mind
or verbal, then stop and remember how you would speak to
someone that you *truly* and *deeply* love and care for.
Be the person that is the most loved and respected by **you**!
Be the one who trusts *you* more than anyone ever could!
Be your own best friend!
If you can spend any length of time in your own company and
love your own company, then you know you are on the right
path. You're the one who has to live with yourself. Make it a
happy life!

Begin the steps for loving and respecting yourself enough to
be *who* you are. Be brave enough to be your true self. When
you are your true self, you attract the right people in your
life, and you don't have to make any effort of pretence!
Accept yourself and know that you are amazing!
When you are true to yourself about who you are without
any masking or pretence, then you feel most comfortable. If
you pretend to be someone you're not, then you won't feel
comfortable within yourself.

This is important. You must love yourself! You must respect
yourself! You are just as valuable as the next person.
I cannot emphasise the importance of loving and respecting
yourself. It is a vital piece of the puzzle.

So, let us begin with this affirmation: -

"I love and respect myself." Genuinely believe this statement!
Place both hands on your chest (one hand on top of the other) and breathe in love. Just know that this is what your energy body *is*! Just pure love! So, connect with your energy being and bring in the joint "veins" of all parts of you. Bring the love together! You chose to come into this vessel, on this planet for a reason! It is important to love, value and respect that decision that you made.
Know that love is unconditional. It isn't about the shape of body you have; the type of job you have; the type of education you have, etc. Just love yourself anyway!

Success is pure and utter love and joy within!

Really feel the love for yourself and really know that you respect yourself enough to only accept loving and comforting words. Everything else can visually go into an imagined garbage bin and be karted away.

Now try this affirmation: -

"I am amazing." It is true! Feel the excitement of that. Really know that you are amazing!
We are *all* amazing! We just need to see that we all have our unique contribution to Earth and to one another. Even if

you depend on others, it is a valuable experience for *others* in order for *them* to grow and evolve. We are all perfectly imperfect for a greater reason! How do we grow and evolve if we come here with complete perfections? There would be nothing to build upon!

So, you are amazing! If anyone else tells you anything else, then it is not true. It is simply recognising this! We all have our place in this world.

Now try this one whilst <u>standing tall</u>: -
"I am calm and confident." Say this multiple times, daily. Believe it and continue to say it.
If you need more "oomph" on the confidence, then try this one: -
"I am strong and confident!" Now feel that strength! Just know that you are mentally strong. Believe in your power. The mind is powerful, just look at body builders. It isn't the muscle on its own lifting that weight! It takes the strength of the mind to lift it with all of the might they have in their mind. That is the perfect example of the phrase "the stronger the mind, the stronger the body." It is very demonstrative!

The mind holds the intention of everything, from the movement of a muscle to every thought and action.
Our minds are more powerful than we can even imagine. Everything is within it. The power to heal; the power to

imagine; the power to create; the power to do anything we choose to if we work towards it with powerful intention!

Try this one: -
"I am so happy and grateful."
Hold onto your solar plexus with both hands and tell yourself that you are happy and grateful for all of the good things in your life. Feel the gratitude. Feel all of the happiness that you can create right at this moment.

This all works on intention, thought, feeling and action!
I have given you samples of powerful affirmations. You can recreate who you are by repeating the words of how and who you wish to be by repeating affirmations on a daily basis, with the positive feeling behind it and the belief that it is already true. If you take action, even if it is in the act of visualisation of action, then your mind will begin to believe it. Never give up on the daily affirmations. You will notice changes in you, even if it is subtle to begin with.

Just remember that you have exactly the same right as everyone else on this planet.

The Law of Attraction

Life is most exciting when we are creating and experiencing with an "unlimited, can-do mind-set."
Your mind holds either "limitation" or "freedom."
You are the master of who and how you wish your mind to be.

We are what we think, say and do.
Everything manifests from thought, word and action.
We work with our energy and attract (pull in) more of what we "put out."
When I perform Reiki, it is healing the energy body that has been manifesting with thought, word and action.

Affirmations; thoughts and words of gratitude; self-belief & love; good, loving self-talk; general positive actions, responses and perceptions - are creating a lovely inner world, which attracts more of the same *from* our "outer world."

"The Law of Attraction," is about attracting what we are "putting out."
We attract everything that is on the same frequency as our own frequency, so it is important to hold good energy!
If we don't have happiness and harmony in our inner world, then no-*thing* would bring genuine happiness.

I would always say that it is vital to work on your internal happiness, confidence and balance, before looking at other aspects. This way you also bring about a better frequency of energy, which will continue to bring more of that good *feeling* towards you!

Like-attracts-like, so if you aren't happy, you can imagine *that* frequency you're vibrating in and what it will attract. Happiness and wellbeing is an absolute priority for an amazing foundation to build on.

Some people believe that money brings more power, but I believe that the greater our humility and genuine happiness, the greater our lives will be for us as individuals, whether we have a little, or a lot of money! Internal joy brings more value than money! Now, I'm not saying that money isn't good. Money is an energy that can buy things that bring a great standard of living. I'm just saying that it is vital to work on your internal world initially; then if it is the standard of living you're seeking to improve – this will come with such a lovely frequency for you. If your energy is in a lovely, high, happy frequency, then you'll even be attracting the lovely things *quicker*.

If you know that "things" usually become a *novelty* and that the excitement of it all can wear off in good time, then you will see the value of internal happiness.

Money isn't an evil thing. It has been created (by humans) as a trade, so that we can use our skills in order to trade for the money which enables us to trade for food, water and shelter.

Some people have given us the impression that money brings power and leadership, but this is simply a perception we choose to hold. We have more freedom than we realise. If someone thinks that they are "above everyone else" simply because they have more money, then they will be saddened to discover that this simply isn't true at one time or another. When people have love and respect for themselves, they only accept the best for themselves, which reflects outwardly (attracting the same in return). I think that so long as we retain humility and compassion along with our happiness, then money is simply an energy that we can choose to have an abundance of.

If you remember that money is simply an *energy* and a *trade*, then we can clear all negative beliefs of money and attract it easier.

Money isn't the be-all-and-end-all, however. Let us look at some of the great Buddhists who have a happy and contented life and lead by such wonderful example. Their way of life is beautiful, as they respect and love all nature, living with such humility.

Some people love the "off-grid" lifestyle, in nature, living in a natural way. This is certainly an example of internal happiness without the need for the temporary novelty of materialism and constant demand for it.

Just remember that food, water, air and land is actually meant to be free to us. It is the gift of the Earth. These natural sources have been manipulated to be monetised in order to gain control for a sense of ease.

Control systems have been created by monetising the things that are actually free. Humans have created a method of education and work, that creates the circulation of money. It brings a sense of safety and security when we work to earn money in order to purchase homes, food, water, electricity, shelter, comforts and entertainments. The rich get richer by these systems and the main workforce are controlled to continue to feed this ancient, yet modern version of the Robin-Hood like mentality.

Many people work long hours, getting tired, just hoping for the pension they have been aiming for. The saying goes that we work hard during our younger years simply to exist, until we reach pension age, when all of our money goes into our health care.

Most of the developed world is born into this system of *existing*, which hasn't been our fault.

I would like to add that I don't believe that "bad" people exist, but this is contradictory to some. I personally hold the value that it is just about the mind-programming people have been conditioned into or have chosen for themselves. Some people are happy and joyous, whilst others are angry or upset; it's our response to things, it's how we deal with things. One person may not know how to respond to their own anger for example. Then there are people who are mentally unwell or unbalanced. Everyone has their "survival" behaviours too.

We all learn and grow at different rates, with different levels of awareness. When we are children, we can lash out physically with anger, jealousy or frustration. Some children don't know how to deal with their emotions or don't have the influential peers for a positive upbringing.

Most people in the developed world have learnt to control their negative emotions and to use responses that involve diplomacy or mediation. The problem is holding negative thought and emotion within.

Once we have awareness of thought and emotion, we can change perceptions and behaviours.

It is important to have balance; to live for now; and to attract the energy of the Universe that we choose.

It is never too late to change anything once we have awareness!

When you know that everything is energy and that we are here to play with that energy, then you can manipulate and change *anything* in your life.

What you want in life is *your* choice.

Just remember that everything is energy, so we attract the energy that we choose.

If you wish to use the Law-of-Attraction for an abundance of money (once you have worked on your healthy inner world), then your affirmations work similarly.

Create the affirmation and allow the reality of that thought to connect with the Universal Energy in order to have this develop.

Examples of these affirmations can be: -

"I am so financially rich that I am unlimited in my finances!"

"I am a huge money magnet!"

Feel the excitement behind those words and add visualisation. Some people use vision boards to match their words and thoughts, which I'm sure many have seen. These are literally boards that hold images/photos of things that you wish to stare at in order to aid the attraction of what your mind is seeing.

Regular action that makes your mind and body believe what words and visions you are attracting, enhances that force.

An example of a daily process, using the Law of Attraction: -

If you wish to work on attracting anything in a powerful way, then take around fifteen minutes per day in a particular room that is selected for your "Law of Attraction" times. For me this is my spare room. For some it's a shed, summerhouse or even a van or motorhome. I wouldn't say there's any rule. Use vision boards if you need help to see what you visualise as having. Place images of what you wish to have on a wall or moveable board.

Take the scene you have set and create an uplifted feeling before beginning the fifteen-minute session.

Before you begin these sessions, calculate what it is you want. If you simply want happiness (which is the greatest gift), then take a photo of yourself grinning or laughing broadly and place this in view, or just know that you are strong enough to smile at yourself in a good mirror for that length of time. Know that you are worthy of happiness and believe that you already have it.

Work out the affirmation that is associated, I.E. "I am happy in every way."

Lift your vibration before starting your fifteen-minute process, as it is important to attract with a positive and strongly passionate vibration. If this is by listening to a song that gets you feeling uplifted, then that is a great example. Then it is literally spending those fifteen minutes repeating words in your mind, and out loud, feeling the excitement and happiness of it whilst visualising it all too. Use phrases that begin with "I am" or "I have", to enhance the belief that you already have it! The mind works on the present time with great power. Always be in the "NOW."

The truth is that we can attract what we wish.

I have simply discovered that our words, thoughts, feelings and actions can heal our minds and bodies, so to succeed in good health and happiness is already the greatest gift I have ever received.

If you conquer your happiness-success, then think big and conquer the world given our amazing creation!

We are here to create, so create!

Set your intentions for who you wish to be and how you wish to live your life. Make a list and calculate your affirmations from that. Think as big as you like!   Always ensure however that everything is always in positivity, love and respect for yourself.

Be an inspirer to others with your newfound happiness and confidence.   When others see you as happy and confident, it reflects, so that you can be an amazing inspirer once you begin to practice the new habits!

New habits come in simply by taking that first step and intending to act upon it daily. It will become a reality if you are consistent and doing it correctly.

I will get further into the subject of energy later on, but our thoughts are very real, and the Universal Energy does act upon them.

By placing a *feeling* with a *thought*, the universe will work swifter. Take action or visualise yourself as you are affirming, and you will create powerfully!

If I can create my mind set from the state I was in, then it demonstrates the power of the mind!

With any affirmation, please ensure that you always focus on what you *do* **want. Do not focus on what you don't want!**

With what you *do* want however, attempt to use it in the **present tense**, such as the ones I've already given an example of. This is important. When people attempt to create/manifest changes in their lives, they often focus on what they don't want.

Again, the right way to begin a phrase would be to say, "I am ..." Believe in what you are saying in the present moment!

Then feel a positive emotion behind it, such as the *feeling* of gratitude. Feel the excitement of that affirmation!
Act out what you tell yourself to enhance the phrase and belief. For example, if you are telling yourself, you are extremely rich then act as if you are rich, by giving to the poor a little more, or visualising the act of purchasing that amazing item or situation.

You simply need to repeat affirmations, either out loud in your own private space, or over and over in your head like a record playing.

Go through it and see yourself successful at the other side.

It is so vital to be aware of our thoughts and words. If we keep telling ourselves things such as:
"I can't afford it."
"I can't do that."
"I'll never be rich."
"I'll never get better."
"I'm depressed."
"I'm always ill."
"I'll always be like this."
... Then you'll always receive the things you are saying and believing.

Do you get an uncomfortable feeling with any of these statements? It's good if you do, as then you know your mind and body is speaking to you, telling you that it isn't good to think these thoughts.

If you think or say these things to yourself or others, then don't forget that your subconscious mind will believe it all and act it out. Thoughts and words are a very real energy, so you will also be attracting the same energy.
It doesn't need to be a vicious circle, as change begins in the present time! You can become very aware of your thoughts and words and stop yourself!

Only think and say good, comforting, positive words that will comfort and enhance your life!
Thoughts and words such as:

"I am always super well and extremely calm."
 "I can handle this."
"I've done this before."
"I can beat this with the right thoughts and actions."
"I am happy and vibrant and love my life."
"I can change anything I choose to change, right now.!"
"I am wonderful."
"Life is magical."

I'm sure you only want the best out of this life. Every day is a blessing and needs to be lived, knowing that it is only the present that exists.

There are so many phrases that confirm that the Law of Attraction is something that has always existed, perhaps with different terms and labels. They all say the same thing: -

-Ask and you shall receive.

-Ask - Believe – Receive.

-Thought, word and deed.

Be aware of the common phrases and words that you use.
Your words will genuinely attract more of **that**.
AWARENESS is absolute KEY!
I was aware of the fact that my common phrases attracted more of the same. My common phrases were: -

"That's weird."
"Argh!"
"So frustrating."
"Ah, for f-sake."
"Oh no."
"So annoying."
"Why does this keep happening?"

"What am I doing wrong?"
"Why does this keep happening?"
"Bloody typical."
"I may be paranoid, but…"
"What now?"

The feelings associated with those words bring frustration, confusion and negativity.
I also noticed that when we apologise all of the time, it shows a lack of belief in the self, almost as if we are giving our power away! I learnt to say "thank you" more so and to learn only to apologise when we truly know we need to.

Once I was aware of my common phrases, I swiftly adjusted them to words such as: -

"How interesting."
"That's magic!"
"Oh, I can make this better."
"Why do things go so wonderfully right for me?"
"I am so fortunate."
"I am amazing."
"I am so fortunate."
"Life is so wonderful and adventurous."
"Oh, I've got another opportunity to do that better this time."
"I can do this."

"I've got plenty of time."

The words that I use here bring excitement and encouragement to me. Passion and *amazement* is a strong feeling to have.

The ultimate strength is to have the good feeling and to believe what you're saying. It takes practice to avert your words or common phrases with belief behind them, but it is reprogramming your inner world to manifest your outer world. What happens within, attracts the same towards you. **The Universe listens to everything!**

Some people say that it's not about the words, it is about the behaviours. I agree with changing our behaviours as well, but like to start with the thoughts and words, as the source is there! I have witnessed for myself that it is amazingly powerful to have the right words, thoughts and feelings and to work on them, until your subconscious mind responds automatically. At first it is a plaster, or bandage, that builds to become a way of life. The mind is incredibly powerful, so this is where we all need to begin – with the reprogramming. Choose your thoughts and words more frequently than you choose your clothing, your meal plan or any daily choice and you'll find amazing results in your behaviours anyway!

Common behaviours...

Habit and behaviour is important too as I previously stated. If there is a habit, routine or behaviour that makes you feel uncomfortable in any shape of form, then change it. People think it's difficult to change habits, as we often get stuck in our ways for years and years, but it is actually quite easy! It is all simply a **deliberate choice.** I've made some small changes to some of my behaviours and routines and made significant improvements in my life.

The obvious change was my daily thought-pattern, to hold that positive attitude, with love and respect for myself.

I have improved flexibility and strength of my body when I realised some simple movements were getting harder in my now-40's. The flexibility took five minutes per day, with a tricky start, but swift improvements. I already had strength, but improvements can come really quickly too!

I reduced some excess fat from my body when I realised we don't need to eat as much once we are fully grown! I eat healthily, with density, but less unnecessary quantity.

I've tried to see family members more frequently, as I have become more grateful for their presence in this life.

Simple changes in habits and routines can get big achievements fulfilled!

Running a marathon is a gradual progression of practice. People can't just get up and run one without regular and progressive practice.

~ 110 ~

Writing a book can be completed by a page a day!
A new career can begin with an hour per day studying online!

Some of the traditional sayings are very true: -
*You can do whatever you set your mind on.
*The stronger the mind, the stronger the body.
*Strengthen the body and the mind will follow.
*Where there's a will, there's a way.
*If you've got the determination to do something, then you can succeed.
*You're only as strong as your mind is.
*What you put in - you get out.
*Where there's a will, there is a way!
*"You don't have to see the whole staircase, but to just take the first step." Little steps per day can complete a staircase climb.

This is my phrase:
"All talk and no action will only bring dissatisfaction."

These phrases all dictate that the mind is the starting point for changes.
We all place unnecessary difficulties upon ourselves at times.
If we aren't literally in a confined prison, then we have freedom!

Life is meant to be joyful! If you don't have joy then something isn't in alignment. Look at who and what you are investing your 'currency of time' in and calculate if these people, jobs, habits, routines are what make you feel joyous. If there is something or someone you are 'wasting' your time on, then work out what is more valuable for your time-currency. Take responsibility for your own life. We are all responsible for every single choice we make!

I believe that everything begins with *us*. With every external factor, whether it be a habit, routine, person, role etc – it is literally how we perceive things. If somebody is annoying or irritating to you, then ask yourself why? Is it something you personally have an issue with? Is it something that has been exposed to you as an experience to understand yourself better? I can give you a personal example. Sometimes it is all about how important a belief is. One person I know has very poor grammar. At first it agitated me, and I found that I was gently correcting their methods. Their confidence in not caring about my opinion made me think. My opinion didn't count, which is amazing, as they had confidence to continue to be how they chose to be. I gained more respect for them. My perception changed.

Firstly, I realised it was *my* issue that it bothered me! Secondly, I realised that it isn't necessary to have perfect grammar in the "real" world. If we were self-sufficient with our food, water and shelter, then why would we need to be perfect with our grammar? I can hear some people saying that it is useful in today's world, but today's world is all part of a controlled system, governed by a monetary trade. If this person can still trade with *his* skill, then his grammar takes no precedence. His communication skills are understandable for

~ 112 ~

survival in today's world. Where there may be an educational weakness, there is another educational, or naturally-skilled strength!
Can you see this perception?

Going back to the subject at hand - it is amazing what you can achieve, with just a little effort, day-by-day.
Making choices in habits and behaviours is also reflective.
We can change our habits and behaviours instantly. We can stand with better posture for the confidence of mind, which is obviously much healthier for the body, creating a better flow of circulation, spinal fluid movement, lymph flow and energy movement.
Habits and behaviours demonstrate to your mind, body (and to others) the type of person you have chosen to be.
You can literally sit down all day long, watching entertainment sources, whilst collecting a bad spinal posture; a badly influenced mind and possibly even anxiety for forgetting the truth of "real life" with this artificial addiction of "virtual life."
I can see so many young people unable to make conversations or hold personal confidence because they are so stuck in the virtual world, that they are unable to cope in the real world. Then again, I can also see that this addictive behaviour can encourage the belief that the real world is boring and has little to offer.
The real world needs to be explored more so. There is so much amazing beauty and detail in nature! There is so much

magic to this life. Just to know that the energy we put out, attracts the same magic in return should bring so much excitement! Why? Because the biggest lesson and experience in life is all about using energy to our advantage, in order to CREATE!

We create our own lives.

I personally believe that it is a mistake to have the belief that the person who holds the technical advantage holds power on this Earthly plane. There is so much natural magic in this world. We can even heal ourselves and one another with the natural order of energy.

If our main purpose is to create, then to understand this is to take responsibility for everything in our lives. I believe we should be creating for the benefit of nature and the Earth.

We can take positive steps to change our daily behaviours in order to recreate our lives, whether it be for wellbeing, a new business venture, a better lifestyle, a better posture, improving our mental health. We can change anything in this very moment, by beginning *now*!

It is truly amazing what you can change in a day.

It is your life! It is vitally important to know this.

The most important change to make (if it hasn't already been changed), is to love and respect yourself unconditionally.

You are an amazing gift already just by being here! Make the most of this gift by living it experientially! If you recognise that this life is a magnificent gift, then surely you want to make the most of every single moment?

The paths you can choose are unlimited, just believe and make the decisions; hold the passion and desire and just do it!

If you love and respect yourself then this is such a powerful vibration to be holding, and in turn attracting back to yourself.

Then, if you love *what* you do and the people and/or animals/surroundings you have, then you are truly succeeding in the Universal energies you're attracting.
Be honest with yourself about **who** you are! When you are your pure self, then you are reflecting that and attracting who and what you are meant to be attracting, in a nice, beautiful energy.

Choose *how* you respond to things.
Let me give you a personal experience.
I recently booked a break in the UK, but when I arrived at a particular hotel, they admitted that they had double booked due to being uncertain of my card payment. I stated that I could easily resolve any payments, but they admitted that there were no more rooms available anyway!
I was able to check in any time up to 11:30pm, but I made the mistake of arriving at 11pm, with no option to book in anywhere else. I knew that I would end up having to sleep in the car!

I thought it may be an adventure; I'd be saving money and it would only be for one night, as I could sort another venue out during the day.

I managed to sleep on a small back seat and woke relatively refreshed enough to enjoy the day on the beach and book an alternative hotel for the next few nights.

I admit that I felt a little frustration, but settled into the second attempt of a hotel, only to have two nights of disturbance. There was a screaming child in a nearby room and a radio or television blaring all night in another room. I didn't know which was worse, but I stuffed pillows over my head to attempt to drown out the noise. It wasn't a cheap hotel, so I found that it was quite disappointing.

I managed to change my mind-set to be that it was an adventure and that I would enjoy the days by the beach and to use it as an example to plan ahead, with better research next time.

Now, I managed to respond with a good attitude compared to how I may have responded a decade or two ago!

I know for a fact that some people wouldn't have appreciated sleeping in a car, so they may have roamed about all night without any sleep, getting annoyed and ruining their first day. Why make it even more difficult? Just change the thoughts, the perception and attitude!

I also know that if people can't sleep at night, that they may "decide" to be miserable for the next day, even if they could potentially feel reasonably okay!

I chose to make the most of my day times despite it all.

I must have attracted the difficult effects of the hotel rooms, with one being unavailable and the next being noisy.
My energy must have been about frustration from the offset, with the drive, the late arrival and the events that followed.

Have you ever noticed that when you rush and you're expecting to be late, that just about everything goes wrong? Or at least appears to? Yet, when you have plenty of time, you don't get that person wanting to get in your way, or the traffic lights holding you up?
When you are calm, perhaps prepared, with a good attitude, then generally everything appears to work out so much better! By nature, you would have chosen your thoughts, your attitude and behaviour. What comes back to you is what you're displaying outwardly.

Just Decide

A mind-set can be so simple!

Just DECIDE to be HAPPY!
Just DECIDE to be CALM!
Just DECIDE to be tolerant!
Just DECIDE to resolve!
Just DECIDE to love yourself!
Just DECIDE to stand tall!
Just DECIDE to treat yourself with love and respect!
Just DECIDE to take a different path in life!

Just DECIDE to believe in yourself!
Just DECIDE to forgive yourself!
Just DECIDE you will have a good day!
Just DECIDE you will enjoy your work!

DECIDE, TAKE ACTION, JUST BELIEVE!

IF you know what will make you feel better and how you know you can feel better, then decide to do JUST THAT!

If you are looking at the Law of Attraction beyond internal happiness and wellbeing, then there are other books you can purchase such as the well-known "The Secret", or "The Law of Attraction" by Esther and Jerry Hicks. These books go into great depth.

All I will say is that attracting everything you dream of is simply like planting a seed and watering it! Keep working on the growth!

Add Visualisations and the Power of Belief!

I know that I mentioned visualisation with the affirmations. This is a powerful tool.

If you choose an affirmation working on confidence and you are practicing these with the feeling behind them, then adding visualisation is extra powerful.

If you close your eyes and see yourself in front of you as you wish to see yourself, with confidence, what would you see? Would you see a tall posture? Would you see a confident smile? Would you see smart clothing and a tidy hairstyle? See yourself in the confident state you wish to be right in front of you. As you use the affirmation to promote confidence within you, then continue to say these whilst stepping into your confident self and taking on these attributes. You now believe that you are this new, confident person.

Then *actually* dress and hold your posture as you would as this person. Some say, "the clothes make the man."

If your body talks to your mind with these actions, then your brain will believe them.

If you wish to work on happiness (which is the main theme of this book!), then focus on the same idea!

How would you appear in front of yourself if you were extremely happy? You would hopefully have a huge smile on your face and perhaps even the same idea of smart clothing and hair. Step into this new version of you during your affirmations.

~ 119 ~

Visualisation and stating affirmations may be a bit like rubbing your tummy and tapping your head, but you can do the visualisation first and step into the version of yourself as you do the affirmation, with the amazing feeling included!

Another form of visualisation that is powerful is the power of words or symbols.
This works well for me, so it is important for me to share this.

Stand in front of your bedroom (or any room you choose!) and visualise the letter "J" that fills the height of floor to ceiling. Leave room to the side of the "J" to add an "O" of the same height. Now add a "Y" to the end of this word that you have written "in the air," in your room! Now this may seem a bit mad if you have not attempted this before, but just by writing visualised words in your room, you are creating an energy in there. Now step into those words and know that they are within you and in this room.
Just to add that I love to visualise the letters/words in a perfect white.

You can also visualise the word "Joy" entering, letter-by-letter, through your crown (top of your head), as if a lid has opened at the top of your skull, only allowing (intentionally), the most positive and loving words to enter here.
When the word, such as Joy has entered your head and gone into the main part of your body, visualise it in white, swirling

around. Ensure you close your visualised opening at the top of your head (as mad as that may sound!).

To heal well energetically (which heals the physical body), it is useful to visualise your body filling with a bright white colour, as if you are intentionally cleaning yourself completely. You may have come across a similar method with a shower, where you stand in the shower and visualise the water not only cleansing you externally but filling you with a white cleansing energy that fills you from head to toe, with every internal and external part completely white and cleansed. All dirt, which can be seen as greys or blacks, can be visualised as washing away, down into the drains.

Can you see how powerful visualisation is yet?
If you attempt any of these methods of self-healing or personal change, then just note how they make you *feel*!

Visualisation is an extremely powerful tool! It is used in guided meditation and hypnotherapy, which are extremely powerful therapies.

Take Positive Action

Coupled with thoughts and beliefs, it is important to action these. If, for example you tell yourself you are fit and healthy, it is important to take action that will help your belief become a reality.
If you tell yourself you are getting better from some kind of illness, you need to take some gentle steps, daily, in order to take the action to strengthen that belief.

Taking positive **action** is especially important. *Doing* things that make you *feel* good is just as important as working on your thoughts. It's important to *do* what you love in life.

In order to *feel* good and create change, you also need to take action. Action comes when you have strong intention to take that first step and intend to follow that action through.

Let's give simple examples...

It is good to begin with affirmations, whilst taking action to make amazing things happen! Just imagine wishing to run a marathon. You have a healthy body (even if you've had to create that situation for a while), so you begin your training. You can use temporary affirmations that will build you up and be very comforting.
You can take the first few steps (physically), using affirmations such as "I can do this!" or "this is my first positive step."

~ 122 ~

As you build up your running time ability, to keep yourself enthusiastic and inspired, you can use comforting words such as: "it's just ten minutes of jogging today. I did so well before."
Ensure you congratulate yourself after every achievement. Use thoughts such as:
"I am doing amazingly well. I have been amazing at this."

If you want to be happy, then take positive action! Tell yourself that you are!
Hold a smile and deliberately find things to encourage joy and laughter. Look in the mirror with a smile (a real, whole-hearted smile, with eye wrinkles and all!) and tell yourself you are happy. Continue to use the words/affirmations (such as "I am happy.") and add the action associated. Really hold the belief that what you are saying and acting out is true! Remember a time when you were truly happy and hold that association, carrying it through to every day's feeling. Do things that make you feel happy, or what you know would normally make you feel happy. Really bring in the desire to be happy. Keep telling yourself the mantra, or affirmation of "I am happy!" Truly believe it! Practice daily with determination to rebuild happiness in your life. If you *really* wish to hold more happiness, then you will do this habitually. It works... So simply believe and you will receive.
Your smiling face will change the vibe of our body.

The important thing to know is that you are winning if you take positive action! You are only looking to be the best you can be, knowing this is gradual progress.

If you want to lose weight, you *generally* need to change the way you eat and drink, whilst getting more active.
If you want to excel in a skill, you need to keep training and practicing.
If you need to heal an injured limb, you need to do the exercises provided. Believe that the injury will bring an opportunity for that part of you to be stronger and better than it ever was before!

If you want *anything*, you first need to have *intention and to take positive action*! Hold belief with strong, positive, emotional passion.

Make sure your choices are for *you* when you take your positive action.
Too many people (including myself) have taken action that fulfils other people's dreams and not our own. So, ask yourself, if there was no interference from anyone else, what would you truly wish to do in life that would make you feel happy? What dreams do you wish to fulfil?
Have the courage to say "no" to the things that don't make you *feel* excited and the joy to say "yes" to the things that do! It is truly all about the *feelings*.

Sometimes, we all have to do things that make us feel uncomfortable, but this is where our thought-process tools come in to play in order to comfort us.

Remember to be the master of your own mind and life!

The Body Connection

Being aware of your body is an amazing advantage. I have touched on this subject a little bit.

If you can connect to how your body is acting and feeling, then you can adjust your body in order to adjust your mind; and your mind to adjust your body.

Another Secret!: It is important to understand that the mind listens to the body and that the body listens to the mind.

A remarkably simple example would be to note how we feel and act with different sets of clothing. If you put a Karate suit on, you can feel like an invincible warrior! If you put an expensive suit or dress on, then you can feel important. If you dress up really well for an evening out, then you can feel special.
Body language isn't just something that others can pick up on to gauge your feelings or reactions, it is something that your own mind and body will respond to.
If you hold yourself tall, with relaxed shoulders and the head facing forward, it can tell your own mind that you are confident.
If you smile or frown, then your body will understand your mood for the right chemicals.
If you tighten up and hold tension, then your mind will understand that physiology.

The body then responds to your thoughts, words and beliefs.
If you tell your body that you aren't confident, then your
body may hold a demonstrative posture, perhaps with
rounded shoulders and the head in an awkward position,
avoiding eye contact.
An anxious person can fidget a lot.
If you feel stressed, then the jaw, neck and shoulders can
tense; blood pressure and heart rates can increase.

You could be doing these things as the thoughts and habits
have been formed in the subconscious. The habits continue
in the body to represent what's happening in the mind. This
in turn makes the brain believe you're still in that particular
state.

If you tell your body what to do, then it can in turn fire back
to communicate with the brain for a different outcome. So,
as with relaxing the shoulders and becoming aware of your
breath; breathing with deliberate calm from lower down in
your core - then this awareness of new bodily state will allow
your mind to listen and relax too.

Have confidence that your body is doing exactly what it is
meant to do. It is only doing what you are telling it to do.

I treat an older lady's feet on occasion who absolutely hates
her feet being touched. She holds onto her legs and her feet,
which are rigid with fear. I can see that her expressions are
of extreme discomfort. I told her that if she could relax her

feet into my hands and trust me (as I've treated her successfully every single time – and many times), that she will relax more, all over. With attempting to relax her feet, I could see that her expression was a lot calmer, and she was dealing with the treatment so much better. Relaxing her feet relaxed her mind, and in return, her relaxed mind relaxed her feet. This lady is still working on this new habit, but she is improving each time!

This works just the same with any new habit and belief. We can change any perception at any time, about any-*thing*!

So, practice a tall, confident posture, relax your shoulders down in their natural position, release all tension in your body and hold a gentle, positive smile.

You may be saying that sometimes releasing tension is difficult. Tell your mind that it is **actually easy**!

There is a routine you can follow, which is to raise your shoulders and hold the tension for some seconds and then just release and relax them completely. This is to tell the mind the difference and that you can actually relax if you choose to. Find the **awareness** of tightness in your jaw, throat, neck and shoulders and literally tell your mind to relax these parts, whilst actually releasing them.

Breathe easy... It is important to relax your throat and rib cage, from top to bottom.

Don't forget that you are the master of your mind, which in turn will have an impact on your body.

You can change *any* habit or set of life circumstance if you have the true desire to! Desire combined with the awareness that you are the master of your own mind, is very powerful!

Let me give the example of losing excess bodyweight. This most certainly needs you to be the **master of your mind!** Firstly, you need to find calm and happiness. Your body stores fat if the cortisol levels are raised due to stress or anxiety. Your body needs to know that you are safe. Secondly, you need strength (of mind), respect and love enough for yourself to put only good ingredients (and quantities) into your mouth, knowing that it is useful nutrition (and levels) for your body.
You need to master your mind so that you don't give any leniency to temptations.
In time, if you notice that your body has benefitted from good nutrition, then your mind will also take the encouragement from that and hopefully the choice you make will be to continue the good work. Sometimes people need to be in good shape for increased confidence.

Breathing...
How are you breathing right now?
Do you have tension in your throat, or are you breathing high up in your chest area? Are you breathing rapidly or slowly?

~ 129 ~

Trust your heart. It knows how to look after you if you simply have complete belief and love for your heart.

If you can take a moment to breathe from the lower area of your core and slow things down, with a nice slow count, breathing outward with a nice slower count, then it is changing the feeling of your body and allowing your mind to relax. I believe that lung volume makes a big difference. My lungs seem to breathe slowly, so I breathe in for a count of four, and breathe out for a count of six, really feeling myself relax. No matter what is going on, it is useful to simply sit and breathe for a while, really relaxing into it.

There are many, many videos freely available online to calm your breathing. There are also many videos available which teach the relaxation techniques, which begin with the feet, moving up through the body, right up to the top and beyond. Take advantage of these guided meditations or self-help actions.

Getting Out of Your Comfort Zone

If we struggle with mental health of the anxiety or depression kind, then it is important to be gentle with yourself. It is equally important to take baby steps in order to guide yourself through a healing process. It is necessary to persist with a day-by-day, step-by-step, gradual healing action.
One of the ways to begin to heal is to take baby steps every day. If you are afraid to leave your home, then just to open the door and look outward can be an extremely brave step. The process of healing is to push past each step, and to congratulate yourself each and every time.
Let us say you have opened the front door and observed the outside world for an hour. You were fearful yet faced it! It is important to tell your mind that you were very brave to face that step! Note that you were perfectly fine and safe. Tell yourself you did it and that you are incredibly pleased with yourself for facing that fear – a virtual pat on the back. It is important to tell your brain that it has completed something amazing.

You may need to do that same action again, whilst telling your mind that you've done it before, so you can certainly do it again. At the same time that you perform an action again, tell yourself that you are safe and brave. You can do it!
The second stage of that specific action would be to walk beyond that door and walk into the front garden, or onto that front path, or perhaps into a porch! Whatever that second stage may be!

It is important to keep talking to yourself in your own mind, by firstly telling yourself you are safe and okay, and secondly by congratulating yourself afterwards, telling yourself that you can do it!

This is the same for every fear you need to push the boundaries of. Understand that others may not understand! This does not matter! Just take good care and action for yourself, at your pace!

With "Generalised Anxiety" it can be a daily battle for quite some time, but by pushing the fear barrier out more and more in every aspect can bring astonishing results!

Once you gain that fighting spirit, you can go beyond what people do on a normal day-to-day basis! You will obtain a mind-set that trusts you and the decisions you make! This is what you want! You are the master of your own mind and choices. It is all about trusting yourself!

This ties in with the uncomfortable feeling and creating the comfortable feeling! It is mostly about "having a word with yourself."

You can do this even with the nightly practice of sleep! If you keep telling yourself you can sleep and that you have before, then it is a fantastic start to healing.

You can do this with the practice of spontaneity. It is easy to get stuck in routines that we feel safe with once we heal, so spontaneity is a good one to practice too.

This is all about baby steps and pushing the fear barrier.

If you don't struggle with mental health, yet you are working on your general internal happiness, it can be facing what has taken your happiness away using baby steps. I know how hard it can be to face things that have taken you into a downward spiral, but you truly can learn to trust yourself. Know that baby steps in facing your internal fears are extremely beneficial! If you feel this is difficult to do on your own, then opening up your feelings with someone else that you trust is an amazing step.

The reward we can find with joyous events, simply by having the courage to do something we thought we couldn't do before – is incredible!

We need to understand uncomfortable feelings in order to find the reward with the comfortable feelings. So, see the uncomfortable feelings as a gift that is unwrapped! By unravelling the uncomfortable feeling, we can receive an amazing gift.

We tend not to live out our dreams or lives because we are afraid to get out of our own comforts!

One thing I have discovered ultimately is that by working on our uncomfortable feelings, it conquers fear and builds upon dreams!

Please note that if you need a therapist to support you during your "unwrapping," then it is important to do so. Go with your *feelings*, always!

People are naturally inspired by others, especially when we are in our nurtured years.

Those who rise up despite particular *disabilities* and make the best of their *abilities* can be extremely inspiring. I personally love seeing people make something amazing of themselves after life changing events. It is also wonderful to witness people changing their lifestyle with outstanding results to their health and body image.

If you have any kind of suffering and rise up, then you can inspire others! This is my natural plan with this book. If people are struggling with mental health, then I hope to help!

It is important to do what feels good for *you*, in your life! One simple example would be my personal enjoyment to swim. Swimming makes me feel good. I feel as if I'm gliding through a consistency which may be similar to flying. My breathing needs to be controlled, but it feels relaxed and rhythmical. The mind is watching the water, so it is in the present moment. It's such a liberal feeling. It is like exercise and meditation at the same time. This, I believe is why walking is good, because you can allow thoughts to come and go, resolving some issues and settling your mind, whilst getting some exercise, which is good for chemicals in the mind too!

Do you often just allow your mind to wander?

What you do, you become in mind, body and action, so it is important to have positive, loving, comforting thoughts, which contribute to a healthy mind and body.

Our body adapts to what we choose to do to it. As an example, I'm sure you've all seen the person who walks with a badly hunched back, as they have sat hunched over in an armchair or office desk for too many months or years. The spine has adapted a rigid position. You can generally get the idea of how someone's regular behaviours are. The way people use their minds and bodies can often be seen by their posture and shape.

So, it is important to know that it is good to do what *feels* good and is equally a loving action towards yourself.

What positive action do you need to take in order to feel better about yourself?

Take action, little by little every day to achieve what you wish to achieve.

Do what makes you feel good every day. Sometimes it feels like an effort to take the first step with something, but if you know it will make you feel good during and afterwards, then the reward is great! We love our rewards.

Our Place in This World

We are all amazing beings. Each and every one of us is
unique and spectacular in our own way! No-one can be *you*
and nobody can be me!

We are all deliberately here with a set of strengths and
weaknesses. Everyone has their own unique set of skills.
Some people tell me that they can't see their own skill or
beauty, but then after speaking to them for some time I can
tell that they truly *do* have an amazing skill and beauty about
them. I know people who are amazing mothers, or carers,
artists, decorators, athletes, programmers... and so on! I
have met people who have such a lack of confidence about
their skill, but they are absolutely amazing! They just don't
recognise their true worth. Every single one of us has an
equal value on this planet.

Despite the human ability, we all have a "soul purpose". Our
energies are here, at this moment in time, exactly as they are
meant to be.

Have you ever looked back on your life and noticed how
you've managed to get through certain times, or healed from
certain things, or been successful when taking risks?

Yes, we have all learnt from what we call "mistakes", but
these need to occur in order to understand what works and
doesn't work for us, gradually leading us to events that are
meant to be! So never, ever give up over a mistake or a
hurdle! In fact, we shall be making mistakes and overcoming
hurdles throughout our entire life. There are smooth,
comfortable chapters and there are the uncomfortable ones

that we need to move through, using all of the tools that we possibly can to grow and change.

*A challenge is an opportunity for growth.

In a "spiritual" sense, I completely and utterly believe that we are all from the same source. We are all drops from the same ocean; we are all a part of a huge jigsaw puzzle, or a thread in a large piece of tapestry.
Your unique part in this life is just as important as the next person's.
Know your value! Be proud and rise up! Know your natural beauty inside and out!

Please understand that we need you and you need me.
What we don't see, we don't fully understand, but I just know that we are all vital parts of a "whole."

We are Responsible for our Life.

What we choose, we receive. It is important to understand that we are responsible for everything that occurs in our lives. If we know that we are the masters of our minds and therefore our lives, then we understand that it isn't right to blame others.

I believe that everything is exactly as it's meant to be, and we are on the path that we have chosen.

Many people disagree with me on this subject, but I believe that we chose our parents before we were born; we chose who would be with us at each chapter of our lives.

Then the obvious choices come in, such as who we wish to share a partnership with; if we have children and how many; How many marriages; How many siblings or animals to have; which work to undertake and salary to accept; we choose who comes into our lives at a particular time; we choose our dwelling and the paths that we *need* in order to learn and grow.

We make many, many choices every single day such as what time to rise, what clothing to wear, what hairstyle to have, the food to eat, the people we surround ourselves with, the movies we choose to watch, which book to read...

Crossing a road, holding a hand, moving a muscle, choosing a thought!

Everything is about the power of a thought, an intention and an action. The energy world works powerfully on "intentions" and "visualisations."

SO, it is important to take responsibility for your life and master the mind gently, lovingly and with great joy and excitement.

Life is here to be enjoyed, with great love and joy, with the recognition that every moment is an amazing gift.

Challenges, with the right perspective is that of an opportunity for growth.

You are responsible for your perspective, therefore the master of your mind and life.

Blaming others is playing the victim and not taking responsibility for our choices.

Playing the victim is becoming reliant on other people's pity, which isn't a healthy way of living. You will gather more of the wrong energy and then blame others for making you miserable, when you are actually making yourself miserable!

Don't depend on other people's responses. You don't need pity and you don't need to prove anything to anyone. If you need other people's approval – again – you are depending on other people's responses.

Many people ask why babies are taken so young, or why children suffer, or why there is so much poverty.

It is because we have all come here to live as an example or inspirer, giving opportunities to others for them to learn and grow.

If a child leaves this world early, then that child has left many lessons as a gift for the people here to grow and evolve.

The greater the "challenge," the greater the gift of potential growth. That child who has "left" this Earthly plain wouldn't want to know that the parent is extremely unhappy and

~ 139 ~

unable to live life to *their* full potential. The child would want to have left this opportunity for those who are here to see things from a perspective of "growth."

We are here to remember who we genuinely are. I see this as remembering that we are energy/spiritual bodies who are living out an experience within an Earthly vessel. Our energy/spiritual bodies are eternal and can integrate with any vessel on any planet, in any universe to experience *that* consciousness. So, to remember this, we know that we can live to our full potential in this temporary vessel, choosing to inspire and fulfil our destiny here. To remember this is also having the understanding that there is no "death," there is only "change" of form.

That child will have simply changed form and will change form again and again by the power of choice and intention. So live, love, laugh and savour every moment on this Earthly realm, since you chose to be here right from the very beginning!

In order to have a happier mind, it takes the three "P's".

Practice, Patience and Persistence.

Some people choose to accept a label of illness and enjoy that particular type of attention in their lives. We have to allow others to make their own decisions. If you are someone who chooses to give life its best shot, then you are a true warrior! ... But then I like to think that we don't need to fight in order to have the best life. Once you master your own mind, you can have the most joyous and peaceful life! I admit I needed to get through the battle in order to understand the peace, but once I decided to always move forward with no resistance, recognising that it actually takes gentle, comforting self-talk.

Energy

*To know eternity is to have enlightenment.

*Everything is energy.

We give "energy" so many names, as I have already
represented with words of "spirit," or "ethereal."
I believe that we are essentially "energy" manifested into a
physical vessel. When our physical vessel expires, we
remember our true "energy" selves. The energy world is of
perfection, with pure love and joy. As it is so perfect there,
the only way we can experience ourselves for evolutionary
purposes, is to come into a perfectly-imperfect form to feel
consciousness from different states.

Everything is energy and everything is one.

I know that energy is *real* from personal experience, but also
from the backing of scientific evidence.

Feel what you can't see and trust in it.
In other words, feel the energy and know that it is *very* real.
A thought and emotion is actually alive in an energy form.
The energies we send out reflect back to us. This is how we
attract like-for-like.
If you hold gratitude for what you have, then you get more of
the same. If you are disappointed about what you don't

have, then you're only going to be attracting further disappointment.

I have seen many people with a negative mind-set become trapped in a cycle of negative occurrences. When negative situations come about, then further negativity grows. People with a lot of negative energy about them have a tendency to be ill more frequently too.
People can become addicted to negativity so easily.
Anyone can get out of this trap, however. It takes small changes every day, even if we begin with the words, "things can only get better now."
Life is about living in the present and making changes from this exact moment in time! Some people create instant and amazing results, whereas many of us make changes that make constant and gradual progression.
Where I spoke of daily "baby steps," we can change a negatively programmed mind to be an amazing, happy and positive programmed mind.
The combination of affirmations; comforting and loving thoughts; gratitude, and good intention – all contribute to the thought energy we put out. What we put out; we get back! It is as simple as that! It may be a challenge initially until good habit forms. After a while of practice, there is less work required. This is when (I believe), we have an amazing foundation of love and happiness within, and this is when we can begin to work on the "empty mind." If we have generated internal peace and happiness, then the calm that it brings can allow the mind to be wonderfully still like a calm

pond. This is when the energy is wonderful, and we can feel our energy-self a lot more and *feel* to know what we truly love in life.

If we *know* that energy is real and that like-attracts-like, then the reality of that can completely change our lives.

If we know that thoughts are very real and that the Universe is "listening," then it brings awareness to our thoughts. This is enormously powerful!

I have seen people with a happy and positive outlook on everything attract further happiness and positive situations. Have you noticed how people are generally drawn to happy, bubbly characters?

We may *initially* respond to something negatively, but if we quickly remember that all uncomfortable circumstances are a gift for growth, then the positivity continues!

We create our own lives and need to understand that we need to take responsibility for the choices that we make or have made. We can create amazing things once we become aware of this. *Awareness* and *intention* can create such an amazing life!

I have personally discovered that *visualisation* and *intention*, coupled with *choice, belief and expectancy* - is an immense formula for creation. Visualisation and intention is scientifically proven to be effective! The perfect example is **Reiki**! I'm not trying to sell the healing art, but to use it as an example of something that works scientifically yet comes simply from the use of our minds, using our body as a tool!

~ 144 ~

Reiki works using the visualisation of symbols, using *intention* to send these symbols via energy channels through one person's body into another person's body in order to heal the receiver. Science has proven its effectiveness in healing factors and is used in hospitals today!

So, imagine the power of intention coupled with visualisation when we are creating our own lives! Just think about that for a moment or two, as I feel this part is important to express.

Even if you don't believe in "energy" as such, then just know that your mind is an immensely powerful tool for drawing in what you want in life. Decide on what you want and take action by making the right choices for *you*, given what you *feel* is right. Remember that our feelings are our energy bodies speaking to us. Also remember that small steps at a time can create **huge** changes. Time will pass whether we create our lives effectively or not, whether we focus on creating a better situation for ourselves or not.

I know I am reiterating here, but the one big mistake many people make is attracting negative energy to themselves by playing the *victim*. Playing the victim in life is very dependent on other people's sympathetic responses.

Not only does it attract negative energy generally, but it also stops the **focus** of amazing, positive creation of your *own* life! Have the confidence to focus on creating your own life. Don't hold back or play your life down simply for the negative attention of others.

Make life work *for* you in the best way that you can. Life is a tremendous gift, and you are a gift to others even if you don't recognise *how*.

Empathetic people can feel other people's emotions. Our emotions/feelings also reflect outward as energy, and this is where our energies interact.

I'm sure you have all sensed an amazingly happy atmosphere, but also felt an uncomfortable one. We naturally sense danger, as this is in our genetic make-up. Our energies interact and intertwine with one another's. With that in mind, I believe in protecting my energy. If you wish to protect your energy, then it is simply about visualisation and intention yet again. If you visualise a large white light all around you and intend for that light to be your protective barrier, then it will exist! If you intend to accept positive energy *only* and visualise good energy interacting with you, then this will be true! Have your own, strong belief! *Gratitude for protection* in the form that you **believe** in will bring more protection for you!

Intention and visualisation creates our reality!

If you keep your feelings lovely, with joy, humility, understanding and peace, then your frequency attracts the same.

Change your "frequency;" Change your reality!

If you believe in everything being energy, then you may hold the same belief that I have, in that we have created the earth as a simulation of our true world. This simulation is a place we chose to learn, grow and evolve. It's just a simulation that we can play with. So, play with the idea of energy and frequencies, believing in being the magnet of energy and attracting what you are focussing on. Just focus on what you want by believing you already have it in the "now".
We are huge magnets of energy to the Universe, so only attract what you want!

Water is a good representation of Energy.
With our physical bodies, we are mostly made up of water, and water is a great absorbent of energy. Our thoughts affect our "inner water." You can see different patterns in water if viewed with the correct scientific apparatus.
In the film/movie, "What the bleep do we know", it demonstrates someone blessing water and the pattern of energy change before and after. There is a significant difference in the patterns. Positively "charged" water has a beautiful pattern. Negatively "charged" water isn't spectacular. Now imagine that the water (your largest bodily content) is moving around your vital organs (and brain – which I call a vital organ). Would you prefer "positively charged" water moving around your body and nicely impacting all of your internal parts? Or the opposite?

If our thoughts and feelings impact the energy of our internal water, then can you see how our minds affect our bodies?

Water is amazing! You think it is heavy but look at how clouds are formed by the evaporation of water! The clouds can form different shapes and sizes.

Bruce Lee speaks of the "flexibility" of water and states "to be like water!"

Water can be how you choose it to be within you!

Negative Forecasting

Many intellectual minds are good at knowing what could potentially happen in certain situations.

The problem is that looking too far ahead with too much negative vision, can cause such anxieties. An anxious mind isn't a clear, or positively productive mind.

If you have a great imagination, then it can be amazingly beneficial or amazingly detrimental!

It is better to foresee a positive outcome of an event, but even more effectively, it is vital to live in the present moment! The saying, "cheer up, it may not even happen," is very appropriate to the idea of negative forecasting.

Only ever visualise the best outcome of things, no matter what the challenge.

I know this can be quite challenging in itself.

This can couple with the "having a word with ourselves" and finding a comforting thought in our category of collected wisdom.

Our Elders

If you have ever seen movies such as:

Big
18 Again
Freaky Friday
13 Going on 30.

... You would have enjoyed the entertainment factor of magical wishes for being younger or older.
If you watch the older minds moving into the younger bodies and find that their wisdom works well, just as some of us use the phrases "if we knew then what we know now," or, "Youth is wasted on the young," then you can see the benefit of "wisdom from life experience."
If we listened to our elders more, then we could potentially gain much more wisdom.
Our elders can bring comforting perspectives and advice that could enhance our lives!
If you have wise people that you can take wonderful advice from, then it can work towards our comforting perspectives.

Life is a journey! If we think of movies again, then in the movie, Jumanji (the most recent version) – people are thrown into the scene of a huge life-game. They get dumped in the middle of nowhere and they need to find their way through this journey until they get to the end. Along the way they are finding things out about themselves – their

~ 150 ~

characters; their strengths; their test of knowledge and their response to everything that occurs!

It's All About our Feelings.

If you pay close attention to your feelings, then you can do what's right for yourself in every aspect, for an incredibly happy life.

You can choose the right thoughts and actions that give better feelings.

In summary, we can pick the right thoughts for the good feelings/the good emotions in order to achieve a happy and balanced mind and body, that can cope in all challenges.

You can choose the right food that makes your body feel good.

This isn't about choosing foods that we are addicted to, such as sugary or processed foods. This is about eating food that makes us feel well and energised.

With sugary or processed food, it will make us feel energetically high for a while, but it will begin to bring in a feeling of sluggishness and that general sugar-dropping feeling.

It's all about the food that your body needs to feel good in terms of good digestion, good excretion, good energy, good mind focus and a balanced attention span.

Love and respect yourself enough to put the right fuel in your body.

You can choose the right exercise that makes you feel good.
There is such a thing as balance in exercise. There are many people who are very inactive, but there are also many who over-exercise or exert themselves. Balance is healthy.
If a particular exercise routine leaves you *feeling* invigorated and joyful, then choose that!

You can choose the right partner who makes you feel comfortable and good!
I know this is easier said than done, but to find a partner in your life who makes you *feel* emotionally good, who can mutually hold good *feelings*, then you are certainly with someone on your level, and this has the potential to bring much joy.

You can choose the right career that makes you feel good and passionate.
Too many people work in jobs that they absolutely detest in order to pay the bills. I know this is quite possibly the most challenging of all subjects.
I believe in the consistency of following my dreams. Dreams can change as we age, with the wisdom that we develop over time. If you wish to follow a career or dream that follows your passion or desire, then I can only give inspirational examples. Those examples would be of people who have

worked full time in order to pay the bills, whilst developing their personal preferences in their private time.

Some Examples: -

My mother worked full time in the insurance industry, whilst training on-the-side to become a Chiropodist. Once the training ended, she began working on clients during evenings and weekends, until she had enough clientele to leave her full-time job.
This made her feel good – working for herself, in a serving role to help others.

Many Authors have worked full time whist writing a novel on the side, until their written work sold enough to allow them the time and money to write more books that sold, until writing became their sole income provider.
This is finding a passion that pays!

A young couple, working in full time jobs they hated, rented a space enough to use as a gym, which became developed enough to become a full-time business in the fitness industry. I also know of a father and two young sons clubbing together to create a buzzing full-time gym, following their passions.

You hear of these companies that begin with an amazing idea or dream that have developed and performed so well, as it is truly working through their dreams and passions.

~ 153 ~

My personal belief is that dreams are meant to be pursued, even if they seem highly unusual. Uniqueness is what appears to stand out and sell.   So don't ever be afraid to be "different". We are all different, whether we admit it or not. If you have a gift to offer, then don't hide in the crowds. In business, people always mention the "unique selling point."

*Be guided by your feelings!

Affirmations, Hypnotherapy and Meditation

*What you focus on, you receive.

Firstly, it is most important to Believe, Believe, Believe! To believe in what you are saying or thinking about yourself, creates a stronger version of *that*!
It is important to fill your mind with **belief** when it comes to the practice of affirmations.

To begin any change with reprogramming the mind, it is useful to find good affirmations initially. The affirmations as examples provided previously can guide you, but don't forget that you can invent your affirmations to aid you to become who **you** wish to be. Affirmations, or mantras, need to be said to "the self" very regularly, if not every hour of every day if you want it badly enough! If you want it badly enough, you will need the same **desire** as someone in exceedingly desperate situations needing to succeed!

If the mind is too anxious, then it's difficult to relax enough to meditate, but it is worth trying initially. A worried, or anxious mind needs affirmations with strong belief to aid in the safety and calm of the mind. Finding the base cause of anxiety is vital in order to know what affirmations are required.

Otherwise, you can begin to replace the mindset from a state of anxiety to a state of courage, by having the strong WILL to act upon COURAGE.

An affirmation that feeds courage and tells anxiety to sit down and behave, is an amazing beginning.

If you have anxious thoughts that you can become aware of, then you can literally decide to STOP those thoughts, tell them to "GO AWAY" and then replace them with the thoughts of COURAGE!

One of my visualisation techniques was to visualise little people in my brain. I would visualise the person who acted as "anxious" and get the person who acted as "courage" to place a hand on their head and tell them that everything is fine and to sit down. The person who acted as "courage" would stand strong and tell me that I am courageous and brave!

With affirmations I can see this visualisation technique whilst saying to myself "I am strong, brave and courageous."

Another technique is to recognise the amazing things you have already conquered in life! Trust me, you are stronger and braver than you can ever recognise fully! You don't realise the courage it takes simply to be born into a new body. Life isn't "You against you!" Life is about "you working *with* you," with love, encouragement and full WILL and DESIRE!

Knowing this, you can add affirmations such as "I recognise that I am strong and brave!"

Meditation can simply b about focusing on your breath alone, or focussing on one particular thing, even if it is a point on a bare wall.

If you can get to the relaxed state enough to visualise what a guided meditation brings you, then this can be extremely beneficial. Meditation gets your mind to a relaxed-enough point to listen to words that can benefit you.

As a Buddhist meditation teacher, I know that you can get to your subconscious quicker when your mind is deeply relaxed. Within the meditation and hypnotherapy, you can reach the subconscious in order to adjust a negative thought and replace it with the positive aspect. Many of you know of the benefits of meditation and hypnotherapy for the strong ability to change a particular lifestyle or way of thinking about a particular thing.

I record my own meditations (voice recording apps), as I trust myself to tell myself what I need to hear. It is good to listen to some that are professionally provided initially to get the right idea of how they work. It is usually focussing on the breath, followed by calming visualisations, then listening to words that will benefit the mind for the particular curative your mind needs. It is then coming back to the focus of awakening to the present mind and body. I am a meditation teacher, but you can literally learn a lot from online forms as of late. There are many providers of meditations these days such as "Headspace."

~ 157 ~

You Tube holds many meditations today, from different perspectives, such as "finding calm;" "releasing the past;" "sleeping;" "gaining courage..." and so forth. There are spiritual or general psychological perspectives but go with your feelings as to what works best for you!

If you're uncertain about meditation or hypnotherapy, then professionals are widely available today!

Hypnotherapy is amazing for working on specific areas of your mind, by going into a relaxed state yet again and receiving the words required to aid you in that specific area. It is particularly effective if the subject is extremely specific to your fears, angers, frustrations, unhappiness, or any particular need. I feel that meditation and hypnotherapy is very similar, as I did learn the art of Buddhist meditation which appears to incorporate all of the meditation and hypnotherapy aspects.

If you want to get deep into the subconscious, then regular meditation or hypnotherapy is amazing. I personally feel that these actions do need to be regular for long term effects and are amazing for urgent change.

Over the years I noticed that no matter what form of aid you obtain, the focus is to cleanse your mind of the negative aspects and to aid the replacement of good perspectives. This is important to do, whether past or present concerns.

I do feel that daily affirmations are amazing for the long term however, as you are gradually, yet powerfully programming the mind to be how you wish your mind to be. By having the availability to do affirmations so frequently throughout the day, with the power of passion and belief behind them – they can be amazingly life-changing!

Be Kind and Gentle to Yourself

Upon discovering the mind and body connection during my most life-transformational time, I found that the negative emotions such as anger and frustration – made me feel even more uncomfortable. It was then that I realised that it was better to be gentle with myself.

Instead of getting angry and saying harsh things to "the self," it is much more effective to say loving and comforting things. Every time I used anger, frustration, hatred, or anything negative to myself during the times of the heaviness of the mental health issues, I could feel my heart beating harder and more uncomfortably. When I edged myself closer to the kinder, gentler thoughts, the heart calmed ever so slightly. When you become sensitive to your thoughts and feelings you can adjust them to the more comforting ones. You may, at times wonder why it is better to have comfortable feelings. I just find that it brings a much better life and a communicative life for good health and wellbeing! If you feel uncomfortable most of the time, then it will eventually bring what we call dis-ease. This is a lack of ease!

I picked thoughts that made me feel comfortable and disregarded those that made me feel uncomfortable. I have disregarded those thoughts that brought fear/anxiety; anger; hatred; anger; despair.

I fill my mind with thoughts that bring me comfort. Those that bring feelings of joy, calm, confidence and love.

~ 160 ~

Then, I take *positive* **action** in order to have the most joyous and comforting feelings. Yes, you do often need to get through discomfort to get to the comfort. Again, the discomfort is a gift in order to unwrap the gift of comfort!

It is extremely beneficial to be kind and gentle to yourself. If you can't feel the difference between being harsh or kind to yourself, then allow me to be the example of the benefits of the latter.

If you make a mistake and say to yourself (out of habit), "you stupid idiot!" Then your mind will literally take that on board! Your confidence won't be as good as your full potential could bring!
If you make a mistake and say to yourself (out of habit), "this is a wonderful experience that will bring me greater wisdom."
That may seem very cheesy perhaps, but it will build greater wisdom as opposed to less confidence as an example.

If you are ill and get frustrated, then it certainly will not help. If you instead tell yourself you can only get better and just to enjoy a bit of rest for now, perhaps for a change, then you could heal faster. Tell yourself you are getting better and believe it! Use visualisation tools! I once read a book with a suggested visualisation method of a "Pac-Man" styled virus-eater, that moved around the body, eating up all of the little green monsters that were visualised as the virus! I used that once as my visualisation tool and it appeared to be extremely effective!

Patience is something of a virtue and can be a hard one to learn. I believe it comes with going with the flow of life and understanding that everything comes to pass.

The Law of Allowing

Let me start with this set of words created by me: -
"We can't choose other people's choices!"
There is a particular law of the universe that I completely
believe in, and this is the Law of *Allowing*. It is very freeing.

Because we are all born with our individual path and set of
choices, it is important to understand that we have no
control over other people's lives. We can only inspire and
give information from our experiences.
I think that we have a lot of control over certain things in this
life, but we equally have no control over other people's
paths. We are all imperfectly finding our way around this
life.
I am dismissing the guidance that a parent obviously needs to
give a child upon their young years. It goes without saying
that parents will usually do their best given their set of values
and beliefs. We are all imperfect, just trying to do our best.

Knowing that we have no control over other people's choices
should bring great comfort to us. We have made choices
before we came into our "vessels," and we make choices
constantly. It doesn't matter how much advice we've taken
on board, or how much research we've done, we've still
made our own decision and had the intention to take the
action. So, if someone is seriously ill, or injured, or if
someone has taken their lives – as horrible as this may be, it
brings comfort to know that every decision made is individual

choice. We have no control over anything anyone else has decided upon.

This is important information, as a lot of people hold onto anger, guilt, jealousy, hatred and all of the "uncomfortable" feelings. A lot of people take the blame for other people's decisions. Let – it – go!

Everything is meant to be exactly as it is.

I think we are all guilty of blaming ourselves for another's misfortune. Even if we have been part of the action, every single event is exactly as it is meant to be.

When people have completed their timeline of life (no matter how they depart), they have gone through all of their selected experiences and their lives can be celebrated. It was their choice of their departure time, so this is also about allowing people's path.

Understanding Behaviours

I believe everything can be simplified into emotions.

Body language is expressed more so in the **tone** of what we say rather than what we actually say.

Think of people's minds with the two wolves now. We are all collectors of events and experiences. Sometimes we are collecting quite a lot of the dark wolf. It just takes a trigger for people to release all of that on *you*, with negative expression.

Emotions are expressed, and sometimes words are spilled with anger, frustration or fear. It is sometimes just the same as a young child expressing themselves in emotion, as they haven't developed literally enough to express themselves otherwise.

I can give a funny example. Someone who hates their feet being treated needed their nails trimmed and tidied up.

They felt afraid and uncomfortable, so they swore a heck of a lot and gave off a feeling of hatred.

Guilt followed and apologies were made.

If we have a simple understanding of the basic emotions at play and the words of expression, then it helps to understand the human behaviour. We are (at the end of the day), animals!

If someone has had quite a hard time manifesting the wrong partnerships, with poverty and a lot of battles to survive, it can bring out a defensive, hardened character, or it can bring about a kind and understanding version of how life can be.

Despite everything people have experienced in life, they have created or manifested it for themselves. It is their chosen path, and to understand the character or emotions it has built within them helps to understand human behaviours. Some people make difficult situations for themselves unnecessarily.

If people realise they are the masters of their own minds with the choices of thoughts, intention and action, then this can bring about powerful *belief*, which could potentially bring about incredible solutions and adjustment of their circumstances!

Personal Belief

I once worked as a business manager and needed to mind the characters of those who worked around me. I noticed that to keep "feeding" the characters in a bespoke way that I could keep them working productively and willingly.

There would be those who thought very highly of themselves, so I used to feed them with continual praise. If they believed they were doing a good job, then they *did*, and they continued to do so.

There were those who enjoyed sympathy, so I gave them the attention they needed, along with the gratitude for their efforts. If they felt they did a good job despite their belief of having something wrong, then they continued to do a good job. They felt their value.

Some people loved their space, so I certainly didn't impose on them, which aided them to work the way that they felt comfortable.

Others enjoyed good banter, which kept the morale going and fed the humour which aids productive work overall.

I know that in some cases I was feeding some negative behaviour of people's belief, but I was also giving positivity. With those who wanted sympathy for example – had my gratitude, which encouraged them to have a bit more confidence in themselves.

Those who enjoyed space and privacy were free to do things in their most comfortable environment.

The people who believed they were amazing at their work were being fed with more of *that* for encouragement.

I believe that people attract the type of attention they feel they wish to receive. When I fed their beliefs then it was effective in the workplace, as they continued to be productive.

I have had the same with my own personal belief, both negative and positive, as we all receive.
When I was younger I was often criticised for being skinny and for not focussing on my education.
On the flip side, I was encouraged in the athletics teams and told I had natural abilities.
Some people fed my beliefs in negative ways and others fed my positive side.
Upon adulthood I didn't feel very confident about my abilities within the workplace, but I felt amazing with the athletic side.

After my transformational time, I realised we are all masters of our own minds and beliefs and that we attract what we give out. I therefore began to empower my own perception of myself and fed my *own* beliefs! I realised that others were influencing and feeding my beliefs, just the same as I innocently did with my previous employees! You can allow others to master and programme your mind, or you can master and programme your own, for the ultimate experience in this life.

~ 168 ~

I began to think and believe what I knew was good for me -
what *felt* good!
I found new intelligence and recognised my amazing gifts. I
realised the importance of self-love and respect and finally
began to believe in myself.

It is vital for you to recognise your amazing gifts!
It is vital to be the master of your own mind and *life*.
It is vital to love yourself unconditionally for who you truly
are. Forget the masks and know that you are amazing no
matter what others like to attempt to feed you with.
It is absolutely vital to believe in yourself and trust your
natural guidance.
You are amazing, just know that and **believe**, because it is
absolutely and utterly true!

Release Your Negative Emotions Regularly

I personally believe that it is important to take care of your mind on a daily basis. Giving yourself at least ten minutes a day to cleanse your mind is a healthy approach to mental health.

Here are some methods I use to cleanse my mind:

Meditate, simply by focusing on the breath and allowing thoughts to drift over like a cloud. Breathe in bright white light and breathe out all negativity with a grey colour, until the grey becomes lighter. When you know the grey is so light that it becomes white - breathe white light inwardly and outwardly. Then it is wonderful to allow the white light to envelope the body inside and outside, as if in a bubble of purity.

Guided Cleansing.
Visualise any issues as a dark colour and place them into a bucket of pure white liquid, allowing issues to melt away.

Have a shower, visualising dirt (representing negativity) going down the drain and the white cleansing within, filling from the inside out.

If it's sunny, then to face the sun with the eyes closed, visualising gold light filling the body completely. The gold extends beyond the body to glow outwardly.

A simple walk, preferably in nature, can replenish the mind and body, after an entire day. The mind naturally allows thoughts to come and go whilst walking. Technology can be a big distraction to our natural, "empty mind" times that we would have had before these inventions. If there is too much to focus on then we aren't allowing times of peace.
Exercise in general is good for "you time," as well as sending good chemicals to the brain.

Sometimes a good hug and to talk about the day is the best thing. To talk is always very helpful when needing to release feelings that don't feel good.

Writing things down!
If I've allowed things to remain a problem and it becomes time for sleep, then I release any issues by writing the negative things down and putting a positive tilt on it. There is always a positive tilt! If you can't think of one, then just holding gratitude for what you have currently can help.
I have a friend who cut himself really badly and felt angry. He then found a positive thought about simply being able to "experience" that! To have feelings is a gift in itself. Some people are paralysed, or wish to have the gift of life, if looking on...

Writing anything negative down is like unloading what is on your mind – onto that piece of paper. I personally believe that putting that positive perspective on the end is exceptionally helpful.

I usually write the negative thoughts down first and then begin to turn it to the positive by adding something like, "but it's okay because..." or "it's okay though, because..." or "but thankfully..."

Or similar ideas to turn it to the positive aspect.

I'll give you a couple of my view-points: -

"I may live on my own, but I am not alone."

"Today was tough, but thankfully it has taught me to truly be myself and not to try to please others by not being so."

I find that a good gym session is always a good way to release any frustrations.

I used to find that punching pads or a punching bag was a good way to release any negative emotions, although today I am a very calm and happy version of myself and find that fighting fire with fire isn't the best solution.

Speaking of which: a lot of people today have adrenaline from the rush of work stress and then they fight fire-with-fire by having strong drinks of coffee to keep their minds and bodies working at ultimate adrenaline speed. This can bring on poor sleep or difficulty in relaxing when they find the time to actually relax.

As the day moves along, I will always use the thoughts that comfort me in any difficult or challenging situation, so that I am dealing with things as they approach. Positive solutions and comforting, loving thoughts can carry you through and make you feel good at the end of the day.

If you have a solution to something, then resolve it.
If there's nothing you can do, then accept *that* and let it go.

Release the Past and Live in the Present

Only the NOW exists. Be grateful of the past and how it has allowed you to evolve and grow to be the amazing person that you *are*. Know that you really are amazing! The Earth is an amazing place for personal growth. You chose this place before you were born because you knew this.

The important thing to know is that the past doesn't own you. You can change anything right now. The past has been a gift in order to know what works for you, and obviously what doesn't. Take that and know that it was all meant to be, otherwise you wouldn't be *who* you are now. What you create from here on in begins right in this moment. The past no longer exists. Say thank you to the past but know that you are here and now. Release the negative situations, knowing that they have been gifts to expose opportunities of growth. Take the positives forward, knowing that they continue to work with you, to serve you well.

Absolutely everything was meant to be, so if you need to forgive yourself of something, then just do, knowing that it is right to! If everything was meant to be for your experience here in order to grow and evolve, then just understand the order of things in this life and forgive yourself. I used to beat myself up over things until I sought a new perspective of the overall reasons of things.

My personal belief is that we are here exactly as we're meant to be and that when our physical side expires, we go back to complete perfection, full of extreme and heightened love and joy. We come here with deliberate and perfect imperfections. Our mission is to remember who we truly are and to aid others on their journey to do the same. Once we recognise our true selves, then we see the "reasons" for every experience we have. When we look back we can see how "challenging times" have actually taught us something valuable. If we know that we chose to be here and that every experience is valuable and exactly how it is meant to be, then we can understand and forgive ourselves for our responses. We can choose our responses and our reactions to everything.

Although we learn from our past, it is important not to dwell there. I know someone who had such happy times in the past, so felt that they couldn't be happy in the present time. I was always telling them that they can create new experiences in the present, and at any time. I don't think there is anything bad in reminiscing, so long as it brings good feeling to this present moment, but **we are where our minds are**. Have you ever noticed that you can be in the most beautiful location, yet your mind can be somewhere else? Then later you realise you weren't truly there at that present moment, therefore didn't make the most of that beautiful experience. You literally are where your mind is. This is how valuable being in the present is. It truly is a present. Feel every moment.

Happiness isn't about depending on others to bring that to the table. It is important that you find internal happiness and self-love. When you find this, then other people can only enhance your life.

You can literally decide to be happy in the present moment.

I remember that I couldn't initially feel the happiness I decided upon when I was stuck in the condition of generalised anxiety and deep depression, but it is important to remember to decide upon happiness every night and day until you can literally feel it, and to forecast your happiness, remembering how it felt to feel happiness and calm. It also took a while for me to release the past, but once you realise you are in the present, it certainly helps to be mindful of that. It is all about believing and trusting in yourself, with love and determination. You are a fighter and can do it. We all have it within us.

I wake up every morning and say, "Let us create some magic!" That is such an empowering and encouraging thing to think or say in the morning. Everything is magical in this life if you notice it! I highlighted this part, as I feel it is a vital part to my day – that first instance of the right *intention* and *feeling* to begin with.

Your choices are all up to you. Live in the now, looking at solutions to challenges and forecasting only the best outcome.

If you have an anxiety condition, then baby steps with belief, and an "I can..." and "I have done this before..." attitude.

Only use the past positively, when you can look at what you have achieved well, knowing that you have and can do that again which you choose.

Reprogramme your mind to positive thoughts, with gentle steps each day. Constantly tell yourself that you are calm, that you are courageous, that you are strong and that you can handle this.

Mirror work is very powerful (if you can do this), so look at yourself in the mirror when you are telling yourself you are happy, or calm, or powerful. Look deep inside of yourself and believe it, with a huge smile and positive, determined eyes! Tell yourself you love yourself and <u>really mean it!</u> If anything you say to yourself feels uncomfortable, then you need to keep working on it. Your feelings tell you absolutely everything! Trust them and know that it if something is uncomfortable, then it is exposure to that particular need. Many people need to learn to love themselves. You are love! You are amazing!

You are always stronger than you think! I didn't realise how strong I was until I noticed what lengths I could go to and what challenges I could complete. I'm not talking about athletic circumstances. I am talking about the challenges in life that we think we cannot face. If you face them with the right attitude and perspective then you can do it! Once you've achieved that, you know you can do it again, as you've gone through the fear.

If you want to change your life then make that conscious decision and begin with new habits. Sometimes just the little changes can bring huge results.

We often think we are in a prison, when the same habits and circles occur, but one conscious decision can change your entire life. It is simply a decision that we make for ourselves.

Don't hold up walls, or resist life. When we resist, things persist. Just release and accept and love life, doing what *you* choose to do. You can change anything!

We can only take away our experiences in this life. Collect as many wonderful experiences as you can. Our minds are our only limitations!

*Be the mindful master of your mind.

We've all been conditioned in some shape or form. From our peers when we were growing up, and even today with certain beliefs and perspectives.

As a result of this, we have certain traits, beliefs and patterns.

All parents or peers have their imperfections. We are all humans, learning and evolving. We often rectify things using hindsight. Forgive your peers for this very reason.

You can recondition yourself into new ways of thinking. We can repattern or recondition our brain to be more positive, which will attract more positive energy too.

I can give a simple example: -

A martial art instructor taught that the conditioning of martial arts is wonderful, but we also need to remember our un-conditioned selves for natural attack and defence systems. In other words, martial arts teaches to punch, kick or strike in a particular way, which means that in practice, everyone punches, strikes and kicks in the same way, using their favourite, most *conditioned* moves, yet someone who hasn't been conditioned in martial arts can bring in an unexpected move that a martial artist may not be prepared for.

Calculate the cause/Causes of Anxiety or Depression

They say that to look to the past can retain depression; and that to negatively forecast the future can cause anxieties. Forming responses to the past can be carried into forecasting the future.

I say that to heal the present you ideally need to cleanse and heal the hurt from the past in order to move forward. It is important not to "dwell" in the past, however.

To deal with anxieties, the fear of "what could be" needs to be replaced with looking at the "solutions" to problems and allowing positive forecasts with a "can-do" attitude. Look at the *magic* of what could be. We all need to face the fact that life is best when "faced" and that we can choose to make the best of this time we have. Once time goes it can't obviously be retrieved. I now try to make the most of every moment, telling myself that all experiences are literally that – experiences in order to learn and grow.

You can recreate yourself anew at any time you choose, with a new attitude towards yourself and life generally.

I would like to give myself as an example. I thought I had a heart problem, and I had plenty of time to allow that to manifest in my mind. Once I realised I didn't have a heart issue, I needed to recognise that *that* particular issue was the cause of my anxieties. By then I was already a big bag of

~ 180 ~

mess, where I didn't trust myself; I was afraid of my life, my death, of other people's short lives and deaths. I needed to piece everything back together once I recognised the core issue. I started by telling myself that my heart was strong and efficient. I began with affirmations, backed by knowledge and belief. Affirmations were that such as "my heart is strong and efficient;" "I can trust my heart," "I am super fit and healthy." I'm sure you get the idea.

The surrounding subjects such as the temporary life we lead and the fact that we all lose our bodies, brought me to other truths and values about life. These were the new, surrounding "lessons" that I needed to deal with. Fortunately, this is where my beliefs stood me in good stead. I have been blessed with signs that have proven to me that "death" is literally just a "change of form." People usually say that there are two things guaranteed in life – taxes and death. I would like to disagree with that. We never know what monetary/human systems may change. Everyone has a different viewpoint in their belief systems when it comes to life and death. If you wish to read of mine, it is that we are essentially energy and that we return to that "true life form" when our bodies expire, but we don't actually *die*, as energy just cannot die. I believe we simply go home to re-evaluate our new lifeform plans. It is simply a change of form, just the same as the caterpillar changing to the butterfly. With that comparison, some people who work in the caring industry have witnessed people attempting to reach out and catch something. When asked what they are trying to catch, they state that they are seeing butterflies. When people are close to passing over, they are known to see relatives from the "past" coming to collect them. Many doctors have spoken out. Obviously it is up to each of us to believe what we *choose*.

I also believe that what we do here, may at times seem hard, but those times are the greatest evolving gifts and worth working through for our "true life form" to benefit. I really do know that we chose to come to this combination of life forms (deliberately a plural), for a good, loving and evolving reason, so I have learnt to trust *that*. We all chose our paths, hence my subject on the "Law of Allowing." This law helped me with allowing other people to work through their paths and experiences without the need to attach myself to them or attempt to control anyone's actions. I know that we can inspire, guide, aid, care... But everyone makes their own choices, and we need to respect that. The "main path" choices (as I believe) are made before birth and beyond our passing over.

So, you can see that I needed to delve into the cause of my anxieties and calculate the new thought patterns and beliefs in order to respond to things differently.

I also worked on my thoughts, comparing how my body reacted and responded. What I thought created a feeling/response in my body. I chose the thoughts and words that created the comfortable feelings/responses in my body. This is where I recognised the value of thought and word. It was an extremely powerful lesson. Only positive, comforting and loving words aided my recovery. Once I had healed my mind and body, I wanted to continue with the same "habits" in order to retain a strong and healthy mind and body. When the mind is less anxious, meditation is extremely useful to practice the "empty mind." This enhances the mind, body and energy combination of holistic health.

In order to improve mental health that has been caused by responses to life's events, you need to have the desire to heal. Your **desire** to live a happy and healthy life is the driving force. The daily effort is just the same as training for *physical* wellbeing.

Living in the present is the most valuable gift you can give yourself. Look at your present self and notice how everything is absolutely fine. If you struggle to live in the present moment, then I can suggest these activities to help: -

Do something creative. E.g., Sketching, painting, writing, designing, colouring in…! Forget your level of expertise, it isn't about showing others your work (unless you want to!).

Go for a walk or run, or some form of exercise where your mind can simply drift… I find that swimming is so amazing. It is the closest feeling to flying ('m guessing). When you push your body off the wall, whilst floating freely underneath that water, it brings such a free feeling. Then swimming is about rhythmical breathing and pace. I find it so meditative.

~ 183 ~

If you can't swim, then just resting the body in a lovely bath can be liberating. Time to contemplate and relax.

Meditate...

The present is a gift!
Every single present-moment is a fresh new canvas to work upon. No matter what circumstance you are currently in, you can change it! If *I* can come back from the mind-state I found myself in, then trust me, you can reprogramme your mind to obtain amazing mental health. We can all heal if we simply believe and have the desire to.

To make the choice that you wish to feel better in your mind is a fantastic step to make changes. The effort needs to be daily until the results begin to take hold and you continue to improve. Even when you improve, the daily maintenance is extremely effective. Everyone should be using mental health exercises just the same as regular physical exercises.

If you wake up feeling sad or lonely, or negative in any shape or form, then remember to take hold of your own life! Remember that you can create anything in this life if you recognise that you are the master of your own mind. Take the time to work on making your dreams happen. Our decisions in every moment are there for our creations! Life is for us to take! We can all feel sorry for ourselves and hold moments of self-pity. Just remember that you are only doing that to **yourself**! *You* decided to feel that way, therefore you can decide to feel the opposite! You can decide that you are happy, joyous and powerful! You can decide that you will make life work _for_ you! Don't be the person who believes that life happens _to_ you.

When I was younger, I believed that everything that was meant to happen would "come to me." I couldn't have been further from the truth. This is a way of *drifting* and *coasting* through life. Other people will master your mind and your life using that philosophy. I know we need to take the so-called rough-with-the-smooth at times, but don't allow the "rough" moments to dictate your mindset. Keep the "can-do" attitude – always - the attitude and behaviour that keeps you mastering your own mind, and therefore your life. Make your own choices, follow your own path!

Master your mind through times, ensuring you relax and enjoy the best times with the greatest joy; and using the calculating, comforting thoughts with the more challenging times, seeing the value of the experience. Know that you just need to move through the challenging times and take a good grip on the wonderful, magical times. All times can be wonderful however once you recognise that all challenges are gifts. It is powerful to change the philosophy of good vs bad. See it *all* with love and *understanding*.

Anxiety and depression comes from too many negative, fearful, sad, angry (etc) thoughts, for way too long.

In order to heal, there is a need for too many positive, loving, joyous and comforting thoughts - for too long. This is what reprogramming is all about, in summary! Say YES to life and move forward without resistance. Or, more positively: *move freely through life.*

Anxiety or depression is usually caused by a battle within the self. Why battle with your **own** mind? If your true self is of love, peace and joy, then why take that away from yourself with the wrong thinking? There is only one, unique you. Love yourself for your uniqueness.

The mind is an amazing gift! The only way to reverse the battle within the mind is to have self-belief/self-trust, self-love and to positively forecast, knowing that you are the true master of your decided thoughts. It is your life and your responsibility to make the most of this currency of time for the greatest benefits! You chose to come here, so why destruct your delicate time with thoughts, things or people that aren't going to aid your joy, or growth?

Trust in life, trust that life will carry you no matter what choices you make. Trust in your body, trust in nature and the cycle of life. This is an opportunity for growth! This is just an amazing experience. We are here to experience experiences. We all came here at the precise time for a great awakening! There is great growth and evolving opportunity in this lifetime.

Just remember one important thing – BELIEVE IN YOURSELF!

You are amazing and unique! Allow your true self to shine through! Be yourself without shame! Be truly honoured to be who you truly are! You chose this.

How Do You Feel Right Now?

It's important to take a moment in the day and just see how your feelings are speaking to you. Are your emotions good or uncomfortable? If they are good, then that is fantastic! If they are uncomfortable, then start by breathing in gently, holding it and then breathe out by silently saying to yourself "let go." Breathe in white light and allow it to fill your entire self, inside and out. Then breathe out, visualising any dirt leaving your body.

Now, look at specifics and calculate what is making you feel uncomfortable. Try to use the technique of searching for a comforting thought, using your perception and beliefs until you find a thought that makes you feel more comfortable. I like to think that my brain holds a category of thoughts to go through, until I find the right train of thought for that feeling of comfort.

Other therapies such as EFT (emotional freedom technique); Kinesiology, or Reiki can help to heal the past.

Although I am repeating myself with a different set of words - it is good to clean up the negativity that you've been telling yourself, or what others have been telling you for many years. With fresh awareness and knowledge, you can now change the present and create an amazing future!

Do Not Fear Fear Itself!

*There is no need to fear fear itself (as the classic saying goes). There is only a need to *understand* fear so that you can master it!

*Do not fear failure, as you're missing the point. There is no failure, only experience in order to find out what works better. If you don't experience so-called- "failure," then you don't experience the hurdles that result in successes!

*Don't use the mind-set of fear or caution. Use awareness and action.

*There is no courage without fear!

There is a saying: "The only fear to fear is fear itself", but with my personal experiences, I would like to say that there is no need to fear *fear* itself! This is for the reason that fear is completely natural. In my view, I would say that fearing fear certainly got me into the mess I got myself into.

If we understand the *reason* for our fear, and that it is there in order to *aid* us, then that certainly helps.

When we know that the "symptoms" of fear are that of a racing heart, sweaty palms, a racing mind, shaking or tight muscles – then we can calm these actions of the mind and body, by telling ourselves that we are safe and that these feelings will pass now that we recognise we are safe. We can allow ourselves to calm, knowing that we are safe and that our body is just doing what the mind is asking it to do!

Some people like to find several things that they can see, hear and smell in the present, that awakens the mind to the fact that all is safe and well <u>right now</u>. I like to look at nature and note the calm stillness or gentle movement of a tree. Just to watch the calm and breathe *that* in, really helps.

With today's lifestyle, we can get into a state of fear and adrenaline with things that aren't actually a threat to us.

In our simple, primitive state, our fear would have kicked in with our predators in sight. Today, our minds see things that aren't as natural, such as events in a movie. Our minds respond to things that our senses pick up. I was afraid of everything when in my worst mental health state. I would have a panic attack during a scene in a movie. It demonstrated how sensitive our minds are. At this point I was working on myself daily, so with the constant talking-to-myself plan, whether in mind or outwardly, my mind eventually calculated itself from a primitive state to today's adaptations of modern life. Note what our senses are paying attention to.

With awareness, it helps to understand our bodily functions when fear and adrenaline is underway. Talking comfortingly and lovingly to ourselves over the long-term is extremely effective.

So, understand fear, but do not fear it, as it is your mind and body working *for* you!

When I have anxiety with the feelings of fear attempting to consume me, I tell myself that the physical feelings are "just anxiety" and that they will pass. I can then feel myself calming. When I calm, I tell myself, "You see? I am perfectly safe and okay." I congratulate myself for being so brave.

We need to talk to ourselves to console our minds and bodies during challenging times, just as the *right* parent would do for a child.

*Don't fight anxiety – comfort anxiety! I tried to fight anxiety with frustrations, anger and all of the same level of energy. I noticed the body connection to these sensations and discovered that the body worked much better with comforting thoughts and words. Fighting anxiety is like fighting fire with fire.

Replace any fearful mind-set with a courageous mind-set! Focus on courage and bravery.

*Don't fear life otherwise it's a life unlived.

*Face your fear as it arrives!

*See life as a bag of experiences. With challenges, simply move through them with no resistance.

Believe it or not, it is much better to face your fear than to cower in a corner, wondering what would or would not be.

The imagination can be a powerful thing, particularly coupled with intelligence of what can and cannot happen. Everything is usually much better than the negative mindset predicting the worst.

If you have-to face a fear that doesn't bring comfort, then once the fear is conquered – the fear will usually reduce or disappear!

Although I say to do what feels good and to change any bad feelings by the power of selection of thought in order to comfort you - if you have a dream or desire that you know *will* feel good once achieved, then it is important to go through the feeling of fear with thoughts of comfort along the way, knowing that the achievement will make you feel good. The trick here is to **praise yourself** with every achievement made. Give yourself constant encouragement and praise. If you really want something bad enough, then it is best to conquer all hurdles. Can you see how useful it is to talk wonderfully to yourself? You can do anything you set your mind to!

No one achieves anything without hurdles and failures along the way if it is something of a challenge. Being a writer, I think of people like JK Rowling, who went through so much, yet still conquered her dream of becoming a very accomplished author! You just need to comfort your thoughts and feelings along the way.

Let us use JK Rowling as an example...

She was rejected during the first attempt with an agent. What would make her try again? Well, firstly if you really want to pursue your dream, you will keep trying over and over again until you get what you want. Just totally and genuinely **believe in yourself**! Then examples of comforting thoughts (that I would use personally), would be such as: -
*Well, it is *their* loss.
*Never give up at the first hurdle.
*Every agent has their own set of preferences, since they have a particular taste.
*They are not yet ready for someone amazingly unique!

Can you already see how the power of comforting thought can aid you to pursue your dream, whilst keeping your confidence?

Be Your True Self!

We all wear our masks, for school, for work, for events etc., but are you true to yourself generally? Or are you attempting to fit in with others?

When we go through our school years, most of us try to fit in. We try to keep up with the trends, whether in the way we dress; the materials we have; the behaviours we hold. If we do not fit in, we feel like weirdos or outcasts. I respect those who are brave enough to be their true selves... the ones who do not care about what others think. I think this behaviour most commonly arrives later in life, but sadly not to all.

If we are ourselves, then we attract the type of people that fit in our world. If we attempt to please others all of the time, then we shall never live the life we choose as individuals. Why would we like to surround ourselves with people we are uncomfortable with, or to do things we are unhappy doing, or to never follow our own dreams?

If you focus on what others are thinking about you, then you are not focussing on who you truly are. You are only worried about other people's perception of who you are. In this life, we are here to evolve and grow with our own time and our interaction with others, but do not be afraid to be the real and authentic you!

To love yourself, it is vital to love your unique self. You chose to come here for a good reason. That is how important it is to be your true self and to do things that are true to you.

~ 194 ~

Those people in the film or music industry who have expressed their uniqueness are usually the ones who are respected and/or loved for their talents expressed. There are many actors and musicians who "blend in," therefore don't perhaps stand out as much. Our uniqueness is our gift, so why are we mostly ashamed to express our uniqueness?

If you spend time with yourself, you can find yourself and understand yourself well. You can also become aware of the energy around you.

Buddha found more to life by spending time on his own for a few weeks. You can become enlightened with some time to yourself. There is a Doctor Usui who spent time on his own in order to meditate and unexpectedly receive true Reiki symbols.

Trust yourself! In the past I didn't trust my instincts but have learnt to over the years. This is all part of being your true self. Trust yourself in order to *be* yourself. Trust who you are and trust your feelings. This is an important mention. Always trust your feelings!

Believe in yourself! You are your unique and beautiful self. Just as Chesney Hawks sings, "I am the one and only, nobody I'd rather be." This is true for every single one of us!

Collective, Creative Choice

We all make individual choices, but we also have the power to make collective choices.

We all chose to come here at this specific time for the specific experiences, in order to grow and evolve. Every situation has occurred because of collective order and choice. We are all responsible for the occurrences, even if we are not actually aware of it.

This is a subject that some may find controversial, but we would have chosen the current situation/s whether we are consciously aware of this or not.

There is a natural law of the Universe which is that of "Freewill!" We have all been given the gift of FREEWILL. You may feel as if you are not free, but it is a natural law that can be adapted at any time.

We all create with our thoughts, words, actions and personal belief. Passion coupled with our thoughts, words and actions can bring about powerful creation. If one person has much power to create, then multiple people have an intense power. Collective thought, word and action has great power to change the world.

We all have such immense power, yet many of us are asleep to the unlimited possibilities.

More Mindfulness

"Your happiness depends on the quality of your thoughts."
Marcus Aurelius

When you have mastered your thoughts, beliefs and feelings,
then it is amazing to practice the art of "no thought."
If you can have long periods of time of no thoughts (an
empty mind), then you can find peace in the silence. You
have conquered your response-thoughts and found a great
frequency in which to "sit in." Think of the peaceful Buddha.
They practice meditation of the "empty mind."
Obviously in today's world, we need to work with our minds
and think in many different methods.

With modern technology we are filling our time with screen
viewing of all varieties. I believe it is healthy to allow our
minds to drift; allowing our feelings to feel; allowing our
connection to all three parts of mind, body and energy.

<u>Have the desire to live & love it!</u>

Find fun in everything! Kids find fun in everything, but as we live on, we can accidently build resistance, thinking we have seen and done it all. I believe it is an advantage to retain the *fun* mind set. There is still beauty in nature that we haven't seen. Focus in on things, note the beauty of every detail.

I think it is important to continue to learn and experience new things and to keep the body working in various ways. My personal belief is that it keeps the mind and body young, with a continual interest in life. Enthusiasm for life is so healthy to have.

Life is like enjoying the fun of a skateboard and learning new tricks. If you fall over, you have got to keep getting up to continue to have the fun!

Everything is about listening to your feelings and connecting the right thoughts for joy!

Master your mind!

Master your life!

Create... Live... Love... and with much joy!

Find humour in things. It certainly lightens the load. Release negativity. It just takes the recognition of *that* mindset in order to allow the release of it. *Negativity is simply a barrier that has been created.* Accept that you are better with a happier mind. Anger, jealousy, hatred, fear ... they have all served you for the recognition of the need to change something, even if it a simple *thought*. Once you have changed a circumstance, then you need to let it go. It has served you in order to expose the need to change something, but it is not healthy to hold onto that which no longer exists. Only hold onto the emotions that *serve* you well.

I have found that humour can defeat anger and fear. I once had a fear of <u>time</u> itself, as it moved so swiftly, even without sleep, during my hardest times. All hours rolled into the next one. I told a work colleague that I was afraid of time and his words made me chuckle and actually *healed* the fear! He did a funny hand action and said something along the words of, "Oh no, the time is so frightening. Yikes, it's going to get me!" It was the *way* he did it that made it work so well for me. I can still laugh about it today.

If you can find a way to make your specific fears funny by framing it in a humorous way, then it will clear so much of the fear.

I know of many who fear going to sleep. Tell yourself that you love sleep and that you have no resistance to sleep, knowing that you can have a good and wonderful rest if you just allow the freedom of your natural desires to sleep well.

~ 199 ~

Get yourself extremely comfortable, knowing that this is *your* time. Snuggle in... Set the calming scene. Relaaaaax... Ease your breathing and settle into a deep sense of peace. Love your personal time, as it is your personal escapism.
Visualisation techniques demonstrate that it is only our minds that stop us from the natural state of sleep.
What do you love about sleep? I personally love the amazing dreams I have. I look forward to them.
I think it is funny to laugh at my young self, when I thought that monsters were under the bed, or that a witch might tickle my feet if I let them stick out at the end of the duvet.

Humour goes a long way. A daily laugh does your mind, body and spirit such good and is a lovely remedy for anxiety!

If you can find a good comedy that gives you a genuine laugh, then please feed yourself with that laughter as much as you can. Your thoughts are food for your mind, so feed your thoughts with good food!

Learn to love everything about this life. It is genuinely magical if you look at what this Earth brings. Just the amazing sparkle of a clear lake; the wonderful shapes the clouds make; the detail of a beautiful flower; the feeling of a wonderful hug... Things that we so take for granted.

Helping Your Mind Through "Generational" Challenges

Every generation, it seems, goes through something unsettling. We get comfortable in our ways and then when something uncomfortable comes along, it brings an unsettled feeling.

*Remember that you are the master of your own mind!

*Know that *everything* is temporary. This too shall pass. Be on the side of history that *you* choose to be!

*Make this situation work *for* you/use this time wisely.

*Talk to people. It helps to share experiences, knowing we are not alone in our thoughts.

*Get into nature as much as you can. We are nature and nature is us!

*Perception – If you can see that life holds many opportunities for growth, then you can see that everything is an opportunity for great growth and evolution of all mankind. Hold your own perception on everything, as your truth is *your* truth!

*Limit the news/media. I literally catch the one-minute news once per day just in case there is something I need to know.

*Stick to positive and comforting things for the senses, such as nice music, pleasant company or entertainment such as comedy.

*Know that you are actually free! There is a natural law of "Freewill."

*Don't forget gratitude! It brings *more* of what you want, positively. If you have food, water, shelter and a loved one... Then you have a great deal more than many, many humans on this planet!

*Know that you are not alone! Ever! If you are struggling with mental health, then please reach out to someone. People think about you even if you don't realise it. You mean something to someone, if not many!

*Write things down! Keep a journal, or a diary of your events or feelings.
Use the writing method to write negative thoughts or feelings down and then figure out a positive and solution-based resolve. This is particularly useful before bed.

*Send out positive thoughts, such as "the world will heal," or "the right outcome will occur," or "have faith in the process."

*Enjoy bonding time with friends and/or family if you can. This is a time that brings appreciation for loved ones.

*Animals and children (obviously all of us, really), feel our energy, so give them a lot of extra love and care.

*If you feel you can help others in your own way, then it serves us a wonderful purpose. If you help others in any which way you can, then it helps you to feel good about yourself too. This is a win-win situation. I personally love to help and "serve" for the greater good where I am able. I believe that we are all here to aid one another through this life journey.

*If you're not working, then sometimes it is useful to create a timetable in order to have some form of routine. I find that it helps to manage time in order to grow excited about what you have planned to do. This is particularly useful if you do have a challenge set out for yourself. This is what can get things done. Set something to look forward to, even if it's a movie you planned to watch in the evening.
Do what you are naturally good at.

*Practice mindfulness. This is just awareness of living in the *present,* and feeling, seeing, sensing everything that *is*, right now. Sit in stillness, with your mind in calm; eat with mindfulness, enjoying every taste; listen with mindfulness, such as the beautiful bird call in the morning. Awareness of the "now." Watch the beautiful stillness, or gentle movement of the trees.

*At times of stress or tension, then focus on a calm breath. Breathe in for so many counts and breathe out for a slightly longer count. Relax all parts of your body. Have faith in your mind and body. Just trust that your body knows what it is doing. Just know that you make all of the right decisions for yourself!

*Keep the good chemicals moving through the mind. The good chemicals come from good food (including dark chocolate!); exercise; making love; walking; laughing; playing...

*Find humour wherever you can, even if it is finding a comedy that gives you a real belly laugh.

This life is meant to be enjoyed. Live in the world you choose and create the world around you in the way that you choose.

Returning From Difficult Situations

Speaking from experience, I know that it is hard to return to life after having some kind of *confined* situation. This could even be the feeling of being imprisoned by your own mind.

This is when we need to take baby steps and be gentle with ourselves, using the comforting self-talk methods.

With fear and depression (similarly), taking gentle "baby steps" in facing our fears and life in general is productively healing. It is important to be gentle and kind to yourself. I tried the harder methods of "telling myself off" and it just isn't productive to your mind. Think of a child in a frightening situation. Would you shout at the child and tell them to sharpen up and get on with it? Or would you comfort the child and tell them that it is safe and okay, and to take their time? The first method can work, but I know for certain that the kind approach is much better for mental health. I know this from listening to my body with the various thought patterns.

I like to use thoughts such as "I'm safe, I've done this before, therefore I can do this again."

Be loving and gentle with yourself. You're the one living with yourself, so make it a pleasant adventure!

The most important thing to know is that we are all a reflection of one another. **We are all one. We are all love!**

We are simply having variations of experiences, given a different set of choices and circumstances.

It's your life!

Do you remember the lyrics, "It's my party I can cry if I want to..."?

You can choose to cry through your party or laugh through your party!

Before you go to bed, tell yourself that tomorrow will be amazing!

Wake up every day and say, "Let's create some magic today!"

Enjoy your party, enjoy your life.

We can do this! Positive Programming!

Thank you for buying and reading this book.

If this book has helped you in any way, then please browse through my website @ www.ejtbooks.com

The List of Emma Jayne Taylor Books: -

Positive Programming Series: -

*Positive Programming: The Power of Thought

*Positive Programming:
The Secret Key to Releasing Anxiety & Finding Internal Happiness

Other Non-Fiction: -

*The Light Within, Between Two Worlds
*Confirmation of Heaven and Our Need to Reconnect

Fiction List

*The Teenage Defender
*An Alien Poked Me
*Autobiography of a Vampire
*The Spiritual Prophecy
*Eternal Love and Protection

Printed in Great Britain
by Amazon

81738564R00119